Select and Convert Your Bus into a Motorhome on a Shoestring

By Ben Rosander

This book is designed to be an aid
to the do-it-yourselfer in presenting ideas
for converting a bus into a motorhome.

It is not intended to be a technical guide
or comprehensive step-by-step
instruction plan.

Select and Convert Your Bus into a Motorhome on a Shoestring

Published by
Ben Rosander
PO Box 327
Marysville, WA 98270-0327

Wholesale inquiries invited

ISBN 0-9724704-1-7

Cover photo credits:
Sojourner is courtesy of Michael Pahl
The Sojourner is featured on Page 56

~

Special thanks to
Judith Waite Allee,
author of *Educational Travel on a Shoestring,*
for reviewing my ramblings
and giving me an occasional poke in the ribs.

Warning-Disclaimer

This book is designed to provide general information only on the subject matter covered. It is sold with the understanding that the publisher and author are not engaged in rendering legal, accounting, engineering, or other professional services. If legal or other expert assistance is required, the services of a competent professional should be sought.

No book of this type can include all available information on every type of bus or every aspect of bus conversions. You are therefore urged to read other available materials and learn as much as possible about bus conversions and to tailor the information to your individual needs.

While every effort has been made to make this book as complete and as accurate as possible, there may be mistakes both typographical and in content. Therefore, this text should be used only as a general guide and not as the ultimate source of bus conversion information.

The purpose of this manual is to educate and entertain. The author and publisher shall have neither liability nor responsibility to any person or entity with respect to any loss or damage caused, or alleged to be caused, directly or indirectly by the information contained in this book.

If you do not wish to be bound by the above, you may return this book to the publisher for a full refund of the purchase price.

Introduction

Converting a bus into your own custom motorhome can be a fun and rewarding project for the entire family. It is also very costly, both in time and resources. Before you begin, be sure you have the time, money and skills it will take to successfully complete the project.

A bus conversion is not a quick or easy project. It takes months of dedicated effort and a lot of money to transform a bus into a quality motorhome. If both you and your spouse are not fully committed to the project, you can be sure of friction. For these reasons, there are countless half-completed conversions sitting in back yards all across North America.

If you are not a do-it-yourselfer and competent with all manner of tools, you would probably be better off considering a commercial RV.

Be sure to check with your state authorities and insurance agent **before** investing time and money, to find out if there are any restrictions or requirements for converting, licensing and insuring your bus. Many states and communities have, or are developing, laws and ordinances designed to protect the public from us, and to protect us from ourselves.

Some states may require an inspection to ensure that your conversion meets the RV building code before issuing a license. As the codes change periodically and vary from state to state, they are well beyond the scope of this book.

While I personally like red tape no more than the next person, these regulations were written for a reason. As with all safety regulations and code, they are written in the blood of unfortunate people who took shortcuts or simply didn't know better. If your state does not have its own RV building code, follow the guidelines in Publication NFPA 1192 Standard on Recreational Vehicles. (See appendix.)

Table of Contents

1. Is a Bus for You?

You need not be a master mechanic or carpenter to successfully convert a bus in reasonable condition into a motor home.

If you can do routine maintenance on your car, build or repair furniture and the like and repair plumbing and wiring in your home, you should be successful in your venture.

You should be familiar with wiring, plumbing, carpentry, LPG (propane) gas components and appliances, gas and electrical safety, and so on. Not being an "expert" in these fields should not adversely effect the outcome of your project if you are willing to study basic how-to guides and have knowledgeable friends who can assist you.

If your object in building your own camper is to save money you will not be successful if you have to hire the work done.

What to Consider

There are many things to consider in making your decision as to whether or not a bus is for you. Being able to handle the rig is one important aspect. To the person who has driven only automobiles or pick-up trucks, driving a full-size bus can be an awesome task. Backing up can be a nightmare.

You may have dreams of cruising down the Interstate to our favorite secluded spot. You park on the shoulder of the one-lane country road that dead ends at the river and proceed to enjoy our vacation. If you didn't plan ahead, you may have an interesting time when you want to leave–even more so if you towed a boat or trailer.

Gone will be the day when you could take the spare tire out of the trunk and change the flat in a jiffy. Bus tires can easily weigh over 200 lbs.

Parking can also be a problem. After the "maiden voyage," will you have a place to park your motor home? Many cities have ordinances against parking buses (camper or otherwise) on the street. You may have to find, and probably rent, storage space for your bus. RV storage prices start at about $50.00 per month. The owner of one of the sKOOLies featured in this book was actually evicted because of these restrictions so be sure to double check!

One additional consideration. Is the bus cost effective? As a minimum, you should expect to pay $3500-4000 for a used bus in reasonable condition. Add to this the conversion cost, registration, insurance, storage and maintenance costs.

Additionally, buses typically get low gas mileage, some as low as 3 or 4 MPG. My converted '62 GMC school bus was equipped with a rebuilt 305 CID V-6 gasoline engine, a 4-speed manual transmission and 2-speed rear axle. The bus got 12 MPG on the highway, roughly half the mileage of today's typical sedan.

Add LP gas, RV parking space and hookup fees starting about $15.00 per night. Depending on the frequency and duration of trips, family size, and your personal tastes, you might be better off renting a motel room.

On the other hand, if you typically go to large attraction events where lodging is expensive or scarce, or to isolated areas where accommodations are not available, a bus conversion may well be in your best interest.

Other advantages to bus ownership include being able to take more than the one or two suitcases, and having access to your belongings *without* having to unpack completely to find your golf shoes. They will be either in the drawer in the coach's bedroom, or… uh-oh… they're by the front door at the house. It is also nice to be able to stop almost anywhere for lunch, having all the modern conveniences, with some of the most beautiful views in the Americas at your doorstep.

Bus conversions are also popular with some traveling salespeople, especially those who follow fairs and carnivals. They often custom build theirs to allow for some inventory, shop space or whatever they use in their trade, in addition to their living space. I have even seen photos of a bus converted into a traveling dentist's office.

Tools

In addition to the standard mechanic's tool box and common carpentry tools, you

should have (or have access to):

- ❑ Skill saw with wood and metal cutting blades
- ❑ Jig saw and blades
- ❑ ½" electric drill with ½" drill set
- ❑ Copper tube flaring kit and tube bending tools for the LPG and water systems
- ❑ Hand propane torch kit for sweating copper fittings
- ❑ 10-ton hydraulic jack and tire tools
- ❑ Metal chisels
- ❑ Impact wrench with screwdriver tips
- ❑ Soldering tools
- ❑ Pop rivet gun and rivets
- ❑ Welder (professional help may be needed here)

If you are unfamiliar with the operation of any of these tools, get some instruction and experiment before using them on the bus. For example, a one-foot piece of tubing could reasonably be sacrificed for practice sweating joints and using the flaring kit on your LP gas and water lines.

The alternative would be the likelihood of making a mistake that causes the replacement of an entire section or an additional connection. Mistakes are much easier, and *much* less costly to prevent than they are to correct.

Which one is right for you?

Bus conversion: High acquisition, conversion and maintenance costs. Insurance difficult and expensive to obtain, storage costs, need tow car for use at site. (Driving a full size bus all over town is no fun.)

Able to customize, all conveniences at hand, a pleasure to travel in.

Commercially-built motorhome: High acquisition cost (but often less than a bus conversion). Need tow car for use at site.

All conveniences, a pleasure to travel in, Professionally built (fewer worries). Class "C" (Dodge, Ford, Chevy, etc.) parts readily available.

Camper trailer or tent trailer: Moderate acquisition cost, need full size car with towing package or truck to tow, storage.

Base camp set-up + transportation at site, all conveniences at hand. A tent trailer is usually easy to tow (even for a smaller car) and easy to set up.

Tent camping: A real hassle to set up and tear down camp, uncomfortable sleeping quarters, weather can be a problem. And bears. You have to unpack your trunk to get to the ice chest for lunch on the road. Some people use a small utility trailer for their equipment to leave more room in the car.

Inexpensive, ideal for backwoods, easy to store.

Motel: "Camping" limited – few backwoods or remote locations. Reservations difficult and expensive in peak seasons. Usually no cooking facilities so you are stuck with restaurants and schedules.

No maintenance, acquisition or storage costs. No beds to make.

2. Types of Buses

There are three types of buses to choose from: school buses, intracity and intercity coaches.

School buses are on the low end for bus conversions. They are characterized by low ceilings, no storage bays and limited appeal. They are often looked down upon in campgrounds.

On the other hand, school buses are more economical and are available in greater numbers. One of the greatest benefits of using a school bus is that they are usually built on common truck bodies by major manufacturers like GM, Ford, Dodge and International. Parts are readily available for many models. My first conversion was a school bus. My next will probably be too.

Among school buses, there are two basic types: the standard (or "dog-nose") and the blunt nose coach. Both have advantages. The dog-nose bus has an engine out front making it easily accessible without chancing getting grease on the carpet while doing maintenance. It is also quieter on the road.

The blunt nose offers more useable floor space compared with a dog nose model of the same length. It also offers greater appeal and gets away from the hippie look.

With the blunt nose, two major types are available. Engine front or engine rear. The rear engine model is typically easier to work on while being generally quieter in the driver's area while on the road.

2. **Intracity or City Transits**. These buses are typically low to the ground and have good ceiling height. The biggest problem with these coaches is that they are geared low for constant stop and go traffic. While you will see them on the highway, for effective, economical long range driving, you would probably need to change drive gear ratios. This is neither an easy nor inexpensive project. Intracity coaches are usually a poor choice for these reasons

3. **Intercity coaches** are the most popular for serious converters with a larger budget. These coaches have large bays for under floor storage and attractive lines. Like school buses, some may need to have the roof raised for desired ceiling height.

Although it is not uncommon for intercity coaches to have a million or more miles, they are usually maintained. Be sure to look them over carefully and check their service records.

Charter companies and the government usually use the intercity models. These buses are generally well maintained, making them a better choice than the intracity units.

3. The Bus

Now if you're like me, you've already decided that a bus conversion is indispensable to your family. Uncle Bill has agreed to let you keep "The Thing" out at his place and your fishing buddy has volunteered the use of his tools and is willing to lend a hand in exchange for the obvious considerations. With these hurdles crossed, it's time to select the best type of bus for you. Buses come in various sizes and configurations. Long and short, various ceiling heights, and have a variety of power plant and drive train options. In selecting your bus you may want to consider the following:

1. Length. Will your trips be for two or for a tribe of ten? A short bus wouldn't be suitable for a large family on longer trips, whereas it might be ideal for a family of three or four. A short bus can easily be converted into a plush, cozy pad for a couple. It has the advantages of being lighter and easier to handle in traffic, which is especially important if you are towing a car or trailer. It is also less costly to heat or cool and somewhat less expensive to convert into a motor home.

The short bus would also be suitable for a large family or group of up to ten or twelve for day trips to Grandma's, or cabin if game tables, an icebox, etc. were installed. The trip might take a little longer and cost more than in the family car, but it would be much more relaxing and enjoyable for all.

In a long bus, you could stuff up to twelve people in one bus using bunks, although, twelve people in one bus on a long trip would be something I, personally, would not want to experience. There are several other advantages to the long bus. More

are available so you have a better selection. Opportunities for creative floor plans open up, and there is room for storage areas for things you can't live without, even though you'll never use the stuff on your vacation anyway.

2. Ceiling height. Most school buses have low ceilings, typically only 6' high in the center isle. If you plan to install a headliner or a sub-floor and carpeting, you may want to consider another type of bus. Some ambitious converters raise the roofs of their buses for more headroom. They do this by cutting the roof, removing some wall panels, cutting the vertical ribs, installing rib extensions and reattaching the roof. Unless you have both experience and the proper tools, this is a difficult and dangerous project. See Chapter 8.

3. Ground clearance. Some busses have very little clearance and would be unsuitable for anything other than city streets/highway use. The standard school bus has the advantage here if you plan to camp anywhere in the outback.

4. Width. While school buses are generally 96 inches, some commercial buses are 102 inches.

5. Length. The maximum legal length for a single vehicle in most jurisdictions is 45 feet. 45-foot buses are quite common. You can go up to 55 feet with a bus and trailer combination. Once again, check with local authorities on these limits, as they may change from time to time. One thing to consider–a 55-foot rig is an awful lot to handle on a trip that is supposed to be a vacation.

Because these standards change from time to time, if you are uncertain about the legality of converting your chosen coach, contact your state's Department of Motor Vehicles or the Highway Patrol. A good definition of misery could well be "spending $10,000 on a 20,000 lb. bus conversion that you can't take out of your driveway."

6. Automatic or stick shift. An automatic transmission, while generally offering a smoother pick-up and being easier to operate, is fairly well known as a cause of increased fuel consumption. If you and your spouse can handle a stick shift, it may be worth your while.

7. Rear axle. My old GMC was equipped with a two-speed rear axle which made it more versatile.

8. Governors and other limitations. Many school buses have governors which limit them to ~60 miles per hour. Others have natural speed limitations due to gearing and rear end rations. While this is plenty fast in a full size bus, if getting there quick is an issue, be sure to ask the salesman about highway gearing. **Gearing will also have a major impact on fuel economy.**

9. Gas or diesel. The diesel is more economical to operate, although a diesel engine can add two thousand dollars or more to the cost of the bus, money you could have used in the conversion. And you can go a lot of miles on $2000 worth of gas!

10. Intracity buses. Unless you own your own oil well, stay away from intracity buses. They are geared for low speeds and frequent stops and consequently get poor gas mileage. The few dollars you might save in the initial purchase price will put you on a first name basis with the Chairman of the Board of your favorite oil company.

11. Power steering. Dave Dudly sang an old truck driver song that started, "All you big and burly men who roll the trucks along..." Well, there's a reason they were "big and burly" – they probably didn't have power steering. Buses, like other heavy trucks, are large, cumbersome and difficult to maneuver. Driving down the Interstate is easy enough, but sooner ro later, you will encounter city streets, congestion and switchbacks. You need power steering.

Checklist

As with any vehicle, a beautiful body may draw your attention away from serious drive train defects. Failure to carefully inspect the entire bus is a costly mistake.

Before you go out to look at buses, make a checklist. It may include the items I will discuss as well as some of your own ideas. Feel free to photocopy the sample checklist on Page 10, if you wish. When you find something wrong, write it down. It will assist you in assessing the vehicle giving you an idea of the repair costs, as well as being a valuable tool when dickering with the owner should you decide to buy the bus.

Features to look for in bus selection are the same things you would check in selecting a used car, but it's easier. Although there is more area to look at, there is generally more room in which to make the inspections. For instance, you don't need a lift or a jack to check out the underside. Just scoot under and sit up.

1. Overall first impression. Look at the body for evidence of excessive corrosion and bodywork. Does the body seem to sag or droop? Is it intact or are parts missing? Front and rear glass intact? Is there any obvious accident or abuse damage? Closely examine the tires for rot and wear. Bus tires generally start at about $150.00 each.

2. Under the hood. Do the engine and accessories appear to be in good condition? Are there light spots on the firewall or lines or wires hanging loose indicating that some parts are missing? These checks are very important because many bus components will cost 3-5 times as much as like items on your car. If you see any evidence of recent engine work ask what was done and why. There will usually be a "general maintenance" type reply, or the salesperson may simply not know.

Many businesses that operate large trucks and buses keep a maintenance record for each vehicle. Ask to see it.

Does the radiator appear to be holding water and is there any evidence of corrosion? Do there appear to be any major oil leaks? This one may be tough to spot, as a favorite trick of most auto sellers is to steam clean the engine.

Check the oil. If it is at all gritty it is an indication that there may be something seriously wrong with the engine. If the oil is gray or has gray streaks it is an indication of moisture in the oil. This can be caused by something as simple as a blown head gasket but it can also mean a cracked cylinder head or block–trouble you don't need. Unless you are a mechanic, have this engine professionally checked. Check fluid levels in the power steering, brakes, hydraulic clutch, and transmission and examine for leaks.

3. The interior. Are there any gages or switches missing? Any sign of tampering or jury rigging? Do the clutch, brake, gas pedal, and parking brake seem to be operating properly? Because some of these systems may rely on engine vacuum or a power accessory, you should make these tests while the engine is operating.

Check the auxiliary control panel. This panel operates the lights, heaters, flashers, etc. Does it appear to be complete or have any systems been bypassed, possibly indicating sloppy maintenance or inoperability?

Check the floor plates for evidence of recent removal, possibly indicating recent transmission work. Many buses have a steel floor. Check for evidence of rust through, especially around the wheel wells and the entry door. Other buses have wood floors which should be checked for evidence of rotting.

Examine the windows for operability. Although you do not need all of them, evidence of maintenance in this area may indicate attention to detail and a degree of care for the overall vehicle.

Examine the ceiling seams and area above the windows for evidence of a leaky roof. If uncertain, remove one or two of the overhead lights and check the insulation for evidence of previous moisture and mildew or mold.

Check all lights, heater motors, windshield wipers, etc., for operability. Check all doors, door locks, hinges, and mechanisms for operability and security.

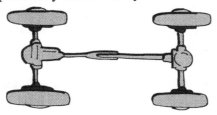

4. The "Great Down Under." Inspect the frame for straightness, cracks or evidence of welding. Check the rear springs, shocks, axles, and differential for evidence of wear, looseness, and leakage. A wet spot on the inside of the tires can indicate either a leaking wheel cylinder or a friendly dog. In either case, the substance will be unpleasant so don't taste it to find out which one it is.

Examine the drive shafts for straightness, dents and evidence of universal joint wear.

Check the exhaust system for cracks, corrosion, holes, and security of fasteners.

The parking brake is often located on the drive shaft. Look for missing parts, operability and shoe wear.

Inspect the transmission for evidence of leakage or recent maintenance.

Check the tie rod ends and other steering components for wear and security. Be sure to check the lower engine, fire wall, radiator, and other frontal areas.

The fuel tank, related lines, and battery compartment should be checked.

5. Test drive. A test drive should include normal street and highway driving. Be sure to give the bus ample time to warm up and ensure all gauges work and give proper readings. After your test drive, be sure to examine the engine and drive train again for new leaks. **If you are not an expert mechanic or are inexperienced with buses or heavy trucks have the bus test driven and checked out by a mechanic who regularly works on such vehicles.** The few dollars he will rightly charge you will be a bargain compared to the costs of major repairs your bus might need should you get a lemon.

Where and When to Buy

For school buses, the best time to buy may vary from area to area, but it will generally fall within a few days of the close of school. Check with school districts about their surplus sales and auctions. If they are upgrading their fleets you will have the best selection.

Unfortunately, if you wait until then, you may not have your conversion ready for the road until after the vacation season is over. You might opt to spend this year building the camper as a family project, planning for next summer's vacation. This will give you a full year in which to complete the project, giving you time to go into greater detail and make your motor home more refined than if you were rushed.

Other than school districts, there are several other possible sources of buses. In many larger cities there are companies that specialize in selling buses. Check the yellow pages in your area. Specialty magazines, such as National Bus Trader and Family Motor Coaching, have advertisements for buses in all price ranges.

The classified ads in your local newspapers often have buses for sale by private companies, and church and civic groups. Watch these closely, however, as they often buy their buses used and there may not be much life left in them when organizations are ready to sell.

Another excellent source is US Government surplus. If you live near a large military installation you can call base information and ask if they have a Defense Reutilization Marketing Service (DRMS) or surplus sales office, or where the nearest one is. Their often sell items such as:

"BUS, 36 PASSENGER: 1969 International Harvester Co., Model 1600-236, Serial Number_____ 8 cylinder gasoline engine. 4 speed manual transmission. Gross weight rating, maximum 23,000 lbs. Tire size: 6 each 9.00 x 20. Outside-Used-Poor condition. Total cost: $7045.00, Estimate total weight: 16,150 lbs. (1) each."

This bus had an excellent body, the engine and drive train were complete and intact, and with its 6'4" ceiling height, was an excellent candidate for an economical conversion. The unknown factor here was the actual working condition of the engine and drive train. (You generally can't start-up or test-drive government surplus equipment.)

Most vehicles are listed as being in poor condition in the catalogs for these sales, probably to protect the government. After all, if you are told in advance that the bus is in poor condition, who can you sue if the d*$&)d thing doesn't run? I have bought several "poor" vehicles and have driven them off the lot. On the other hand, I have seen vehicles sold for top dollar that had to be towed off the lot, so buyer beware. Be sure to inspect the property carefully before bidding.

The above-described bus sold for $825.00 at auction in San Diego in November 1982. I have seen buses in fair to good condition sell for $250.00 - $500.00 at these auctions.

Several years ago I bought two buses in a sealed bid for a total of $85.00. Both were missing parts, but by combining the two, I was able to make one good running bus and needed only a few additional parts and accessories.

My first bus was found in a field that I passed every day going to and from work. I was able to buy it, put on new tires, overhaul the engine, and do a bare-bones conversion for a total of $2000.00 in 1972.

In today's market the least you should expect to pay for a bus is about $2,000 - $4,000. I have seen diesels advertised for $3,500.

Sample Checklist

Use this checklist as a starting point.
There are many other things that could be checked that are unique to a type or configuration of bus.

General

Owner _____
Phone _____
Address _____

Make _____
Model _____
Year _____
Mileage _____
Estimated MPG _____

School bus / inter-city / transit
Geared for city or highway

Asking price _____
Warranties _____

___ Maintenance record available/reviewed

Exterior

___ General appearance
___ Overall width/length
___ Corrosion
___ Dents/accident damage
___ Lights
___ Windows — front
___ Windows — rear
___ Windows— side
___ Doors work OK
___ Tire condition (cracks, tread)
___ Head/tail and side marker lights

The Great Down Under

___ Engine and transmission
___ Front end parts
___ Drive shafts/universal joints
___ Exhaust system
___ Differential
___ Frame/suspension/axle damage

___ System components missing
___ Ground clearance
___ Brakes—condition and leaks

Interior

___ Useable floor length   _____
___ Ceiling height (center aisle) _____
___ Evidence of leaking ceiling
___ Control panel
___ Interior lights
___ Heaters
___ Windshield wipers
___ Floor rot or rust
___ Window operation

Drive train

Engine type and displacement _____
Fuel (Gasoline / Diesel / LPG / natural gas)
Engine—front/rear/mid

Transmission: Automatic / Manual
# of forward gears _____

Differential: One/Two speed

Condition of engine components and fluid level

___ Oil
___ Radiator
___ Power steering
___ Brake fluid
___ Hydraulic Brake
___ Missing parts

___ Belts
___ Hoses
___ Battery/battery box
___ Wiring

Test Drive

___ Starting
___ Gauges give normal readings
___ Acceleration
___ Transmission shifts properly
___ Steering tight
___ front end wobble
___ Brakes work properly

4. Special Considerations

Now that you have selected your bus, you have some decisions to make.

Insulation. If you plan to use your bus at all in the winter, you might consider beefing up the insulation. In fact, you might inspect your bus to see if insulation was ever installed. Many buses have none. If you plan to panel the bus, installing insulation could be done in the course of regular construction. If not, you will have to decide whether to remove the panels for installation. Once the conversion is complete, it's too late to change your mind.

In our first conversion, we opted for utility and economy. We also needed to complete the conversion quickly due to my upcoming transfer, so we didn't install paneling.

Consider our plight on a winter trip. We left Rhode Island in December bound for St. Louis and then Montana. The day we left St. Louis, the temperature dropped to zero and hovered between 0° and –20° Fahrenheit for the remainder of the trip. The defroster was working constantly, and our 30,000 BTU furnace

didn't have a chance. We used a 30-lb. bottle of LP Gas every day.

It became necessary to scrape the frost forming on the inside of the side windows so I could see the rear view mirrors. Frost formed on the interior walls from the floor to the windows at night, and the second day, both of our water tanks, which were located *inside*, froze.

I attributed these conditions to several factors:

- ❑ The steel floor was not insulated. In the rear portion I had installed ½" plywood and carpeting. If I had done that one thing to the entire bus, I would have raised the temperature of the bus significantly.

- ❑ Sloppy workmanship—mine not GMC's. I had removed several windows in areas where none were wanted and installed plywood. In my haste, I failed to properly seal them.

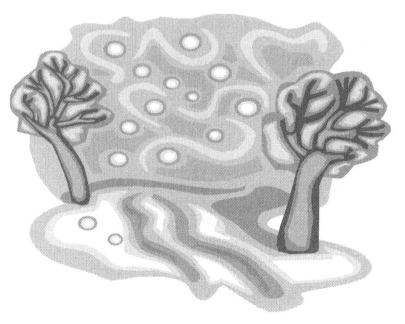

❑ I installed what I thought was a "nifty" vent in the roof. Unfortunately, I failed to select one that could be closed. Even after plugging the hole, some precious heat was lost.

❑ Although all windows had curtains we could have used heavier material. I used standard household curtain rods. On the next conversion, I would use standard RV curtain hardware available through most RV parts dealerships for a better fit with less heat loss. Additional heat retention would have been obtained through insulation and paneling.

If you plan to use your bus frequently in the winter, months you may want to use dark exterior colors to absorb as much light as possible. Use light colors for summer use.

Your travel goals. If your bus will be used primarily for day trips, you may just want to install a counter and portable items, such as Coleman stoves and coolers. A bus used for hunting and fishing trips should have a linoleum or tile floor rather than carpet. It would probably need a refrigerator and a good furnace.

Resale value may be one of your most important considerations. While the layout of your bus may be pretty firm in your mind, you may want to consider options that enhance its value.

Our bus was a long one designed only for my wife and me. However, we built it so that it could comfortably accommodate six or seven. The only thing my buyer had to do was remove the double bed from the rear and install bunks or built-ins.

The extra shelf space we built in, the dining

facilities which were larger than we needed, the large capacity water tanks and double bowl sink were bonuses to us and made the bus more attractive to the family who bought it. These items cost only a few extra dollars to install in the original construction and would save hundreds over trying to upgrade later.

Speaking of resale value, if you are looking for a hobby that will pay off big, keep on looking. **Bus conversions, especially home conversions, are usually very difficult to sell.**

As an example, one beautifully converted coach recently sold for $7,000.00 after months on the market. The owner had $85,000 "invested."

I was fortunate with my first conversion in that I broke even when I sold it. But in doing so, thousands of man-hours went unrewarded.

5. Shopping on a Shoestring

At least two things are clear from your purchase of this book.

(1). You've got the wanderlust, and

(2). Either you are a Do-it-Yourselfer, or you simply can't afford a $50,000.00 StratoCruiser.

Once you have a bus in good condition, you should be able to accumulate many of the items that you will need for little or no cost if you are willing to take the time and trouble to look.

When you are shopping on a shoestring you can't always be too choosy. Some things such as color and style of appliances may have to be worked around, but you *must* have at least a loose plan and a good idea of what you want.

The most obvious places to begin your search are the classified ads, yard sales, swap meets and flea markets. You can also run your own "wanted" ad specifying what you are looking for. Check with RV parts dealers and RV service companies. They often have perfectly serviceable merchandise that is chipped, dented or scratched. They may also carry some reconditioned appliances.

In our first conversion we found a new porcelain RV toilet with a chip in the rear of the base and an aluminum water tank with a dent in it at considerable savings. Some dealers may be persuaded to give you a discount if you can convince them that you will buy all your accessories from them in a reasonable period of time.

Other often overlooked sources of

appliances and accessories are truck salvage companies (junk yards). With the increasing number of RVs on the road, you can bet that there are a few that wore out or met with some mishap.

Many larger stores have discount sections or distribution centers for freight damaged, customer returns, reconditioned items, demonstrators, and undelivered special order items. Savings can be 20 - 50%– sometimes even more.

Don't overlook Deseret Industries, Goodwill stores, the Salvation Army, other second hand stores and even pawnshops in your quest for savings. Additionally, some of these stores will custom make anything from mattresses to dressers to your specifications. You might get a good bargain and help the handicapped at the same time. Many of these stores maintain a mailing list. Often, if they don't have what you want, they'll keep your name on file and call you if the item should become available later.

You might want to send for some of the many specialty catalogs that are available, such as JC Whitney. The only disadvantage is that it's hard to dicker with a catalog. You will find links to several catalog stores on the Resource disk that accompanies this book.

You can often obtain used items free from homes and businesses being remodeled. We were given an entire section of counter top from a bar that was being remodeled, took off what we wanted (we disposed of the scraps), made minor alterations, and installed it. They are excellent sources for lumber, sinks, plumbing, wiring, cabinets, mirrors, etc. The list is almost endless.

WARNING: Be cautious in the reuse of electrical wiring. If it looks questionable,

have it inspected by a qualified electrician or don't use it. Safety is of far greater importance than saving a few bucks.

If you talk to the contractor or workers, they might let you take salvaged items out yourself. It will be easier for them and better for you, since you will be much more careful removing an item you plan to reuse. Be sure to stay out of their way and *bring your own tools*!

Do not attempt to use a residence type commode. They use too much water. Water and holding tank space are at a premium while on the road, or camping.

15 and 30-gallon drums make excellent holding tanks and are a suitable alternative to commercially built tanks. Do not attempt to use 55-gallon drums. They are too bulky. The old aluminum beer keg in the garage might easily be converted into a water tank.

Cannibalize your own bus for resources. The overhead handrails should be saved, if removed, and can be put to a variety of uses. They can be cut to provide curtain rods for the shower, room dividers, etc. They are usually very sturdy, and with a little imagination, might be employed as hand holds for use while the coach is in motion. We also used a section to make a sliding bar lock for the front door. See the illustration on Page 46.

If you compartmentalize your bus, some of the overhead lights and heaters may be in the way or not needed. These can be removed and relocated. Be sure that you properly cap the wiring and heater hoses to prevent shorts and leaks, and so that the operation of the remaining lights and heaters will not be affected.

Some suggestions for reuse of the lights include: under the hood in the engine compartment, storage bays and even on the exterior for auxiliary lighting if you properly seal them from the elements. Removed heaters could be saved as spares or sold.

When removing the bus seats, save the good screws or bolts. They can prove invaluable later. Unless you plan to purchase or make a special RV dining set that converts into a bed, you might consider using two bus seats facing each other, separated by a dining table.

Many bus seats have only two legs and mount to a ledge on the wall. Others have the conventional four legs. The four-legged variety might easily be sold at swap meets for $5 - $10 each. You may have some success at selling the two-legged variety back to the same bus company that sold you the bus, but they probably already have spares, so don't count on it.

Try to find a metal recycling facility for the others to save on dump fees and to be kinder to the environment. You might also consider donating them back to the bus company, if they want them, it will save you disposal costs and headaches.

Carefully remove unused windows. They can be used to replace broken ones, saved as spares, or sold.

1" x 2 ½" pieces of old tire side wall, a washer, and a sheet metal screw can provide mounting clamps for your electrical wiring and LP gas lines instead of expensive, commercially made clamps.

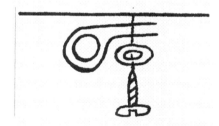

HARDWARE: You will be amazed at the quantity of nuts, bolts and screws that you will use in the conversion process. Bolts can cost from 8 - 20 cents each if purchased individually or in "blister packs".

You should determine what you would need and buy them by the box. There are usually 100 pieces in a box and the savings can be 60 - 70%. You will also avoid unnecessary trips to the store for two or three bolts.

If your bus does not have a vacuum gauge for reading fuel economy, install one and learn how to use it.

One final suggestion for cutting your costs. **synthetic lubricants.** These lubricants can give you increased fuel economy, longer engine and drive train life, aid starting in cold weather and provide better protection at higher temperatures. The high initial price can be compensated many times over in total cost savings.

Synthetic lubricants are available for virtually every need: gas and diesel oil, gear lube, grease, automatic transmission fluids, fuel additives, etc.

For more information on these fine American-made lubricants, check the yellow pages under "lubricants" or write: AMSOIL Inc., AMSOIL Bldg., Superior, WI 54880. Their home page is **http://www.amsoil.com/**.

6. Accessories

The first thing you should seriously consider buying is "The Book." The shop manual for your bus can be one of your most valuable tools. You should also consider buying instruction guides for LP gas, plumbing and electrical systems as needed. While household and RV systems have many similarities, RV systems have  more components and are sometimes more complex than household systems, so try to locate manuals for RV systems.

Another important source of information is the servicemen at your RV service center. This book is not intended to be a complete how-to guide, so if you have a question or problem, ASK! Most service center personnel are willing to give you tips and advice.

Propane system: For short summer trips with a gas refrigerator and range, dual 20 - 30 lb. cylinders should be sufficient. These cylinders are easily removable and portable for easy refilling when needed. With the modern regulators available, you can detach one cylinder while the system continues to operate off the other. If you plan longer trips, especially in the winter, you may consider larger, permanently mounted tanks. Special RV tanks are available up to about 85-lbs. capacity.

Range. In interviewing several home converters, some tended to prefer standard household ranges and ovens to their special RV counterparts. RV appliances tend to be small and some complained about durability. If you do opt for the household units, check them carefully. They are not intended for mobile use and you could find a number of unwelcome rattles.

Refrigerator. You might be able to locate an old apartment-size gas refrigerator. If you want the commercial RV variety, you will find several brands available in sizes up to about 12 cubic feet. There are a number of options available, similar to those commonly found in home refrigerators, such as separate doors for the refrigerator and freezer compartments, icemakers and reversible doors.

Refrigerator power options include LP gas, 12-volts D.C., and 110-volts AC in any combination. Some units are available that work with all three power sources. Because of the power requirements for refrigerators, 12 volt DC has limited usefulness. If you plan to "camp" extensively in RV campgrounds, your refrigerator should operate on 110 Volts AC in addition to LP gas to save your propane supply. Prices start at about $1000.00 for the better RV refrigerators.

Furnace. To select the appropriate BTU rating of your furnace, measure the cubic footage of the coach and compare it with the rated capacity of the furnace. Your RV dealership can give you help in this. You should consider a forced air furnace if you plan to travel in the winter, especially in one of the longer coaches. Otherwise, tropic plants may adorn your living room while you cuddle with the polar bear in the bedroom.

Water heater. You can get water heaters with a capacity as low as about three gallons, but don't plan on any long hot showers with this size. A six-gallon water heater produces plenty of hot water for our family of six, and is the smallest capacity that I recommend. To save money and space, you may be able to obtain a water heater and furnace in one unit. You may also consider ordering one of the "instantaneous" water heaters. They heat the water on demand instead if using a tank. Users tell me they never run out of hot water. The trade off is, they are more costly than the standard RV water heater.

Auxiliary power plants (generators).
Review the power requirements of planned appliances and compare with the rated output of your generator. A check with your RV service center should give you a good idea of how much power you need. It would be better to have a little more power than you need than to run short. You might consider one of the portable generators if your power requirements are low so you could simply disconnect it and remove it for other purposes.

WARNING:

Properly wiring generators, inverters, solar systems, auxiliary batteries and like items can be tricky. If you are not a qualified electrician, be sure to get professional help.

Auxiliary batteries. An auxiliary battery is strongly recommended especially if you plan to camp out in the "boonies." It should be connected to your coach with a battery isolator, which allows accessories, such as radios, TVs or coach lights to be operated from a separate battery. You could drain the cabin's battery dry and still have the coach's main battery fully charged and ready to start the engine. A battery isolator also allows for automatic recharging of

both batteries without having to operate a lot of switches or switch batteries manually. Your RV service center or your local mechanic can help you get it hooked up. The fee saved in not having the tow truck go 40 miles to jump start your coach one time could pay for the system.

You will want a large "deep cycle" or RV battery for the cabin rather than a standard car battery. A car battery is designed to provide short duration, high bursts of energy for starting and is immediately recharged. A deep cycle battery is used for sustained periods with low output before recharging.

AC/DC Inverter. This device is almost a necessity in an RV. It allows you to use 12 volt power for lights, fans and other small appliances. When shore power is available, you can plug in and the inverter converts 120-volts AC to 12-volts DC, powering your accessories without battery drain.

Solar energy. For many RVs and bus conversions, solar power is impractical and an unnecessary expense, although this feature is included on some conversions.

Most vacationers using RVs will be traveling or staying in parks with hook-ups, perhaps making brief, occasional stops in isolated areas with no facilities. Using our standard deep cycle cabin battery, we can run the lights, use the electric water pump for showers and cooking and listen to the radio for two weeks without recharging. The trick is to use power conservatively. When we leave, the battery is fully charged long before we reach our next stop.

For those who wish to utilize microwaves, toasters and other creature comforts, a solar system makes sense.

Additionally, those that camp for extended periods of time in the outback would find a solar system much more of a necessity and well worth the expense.

See Chapter 10 for more information on solar systems.

Air conditioner. Air conditioning is expensive, but is standard on most commercial motor homes. Depending on your budget and travel plans, it may be a worthwhile consideration. They tend to use a lot of power and you will need to add an auxiliary power plant to operate it if you don't stay in RV parks. Some RV parks also charge an additional fee if you have air conditioning to offset your power usage.

Microwave ovens. This popular option has many time-saving advantages. You should check into special RV units, as household units may not withstand the vibrations and stresses of motor home use. Be sure to "shock mount" the unit to protect against excessive vibration.

Televisions. The motor home industry has not escaped the invasion of the "one eyed monster." There are several companies that sell special TV swivel mounts and specialty antennas for RVs. Some RVs even have satellite receivers so the owners wont miss any I Love Lucy reruns while on the road. Once again, be sure to check on TVs especially designed for RVs.

Washers and dryers. Some of the larger, more expensive conversions include a washer and dryer. There are several suitable models available, incorporating both items into a single unit.

Computers, modems and telephones. More and more RV parks are becoming modem friendly and offer telephone hook-ups.

Water systems. The most popular systems use air pressure or motor driven pumps to provide water pressure. I recommend the 12-volt motor driven water pump for most applications. When you turn a faucet on, the pump senses a drop in water pressure and activates automatically. It turns itself off when pressure is restored. Don't expect the same pressure you would at home, but results are satisfactory. Be sure to install a one way check valve so connecting your system to shore water supply won't reverse the pressure on the pump.

Most RVs have **two holding tanks**; one to service the commode only, the other for "gray water" from the sinks and shower. At this writing, however, I am told that many states have banned indiscriminate dumping of gray water and other states are following suit. I also understand that some RV manufacturers are installing single holding tank systems. Be sure to consult your RV dealer when designing your waste system, and don't forget the drain traps!

When planning your systems try to estimate your water usage as close as possible. A good rule of thumb would be to have enough water supply and holding tank capacity for five - seven days. More if you frequently "boon dock". Be careful not to over-do it, though. Water will add a lot of weight to your conversion.

Awnings. Awnings can add much in comfort and convenience to your motor home. Aside from offering some outside shade for your lawn chairs and dining, they can contribute to keeping your coach cool by keeping the sun's rays out..

7. Making Your Bus a Home on Wheels.

Now that you have your materials and appliances together, it's time to finalize your plans. Don't forget to utilize "The Great Down Under." It's the ideal place for water and holding tanks, the spare tire, storage bins and a toolbox. Most of these items can be built in place or bolted on.

Be sure to balance your loads. You should try to have your water supply and fuel tanks on opposite sides of the coach. This will help provide for a better ride and help keep the bus level.

If you are going to install a **plywood sub-floor,** put down a layer of moisture barrier (tar paper) first, then secure the new plywood using bolts with countersunk heads. This will provide a smoother floor for carpet or tile. This is no place to skimp. Because bus floors have ridges and are uneven, **use at least ½" plywood for a smooth surface.** Anything less will give you unsatisfactory results.

Your next step should be to **draw your plans out in chalk, full scale, right on the floor.** Use 1" masking tape on the walls to show cabinets, etc.

"Live in" your plan for a few hours (or days), trying planned cupboards, storage areas, refrigerator doors, even the john. You will then be able to see if everything will fit and if mounting, hookup, and service access areas are accessible. If there are any last minute changes to be made, this is the time to make them. A slightly cramped feeling now will be magnified ten fold when the conversion is complete, so try to foresee and resolve all conflicts and potential problems now. In some "professionally-built" RVs, you have a hard time just sitting down in the john. Thorough planning can help you avoid such misery.

While making these determinations, don't forget to check under the bus, where you will find numerous bus components. Be sure that your design will not restrict maintenance access to, or free movement of these items. You may need to modify your design to prevent bigger problems later.

If possible, position all service connections (water, power, sewer, etc.) on the left side of the coach. Most RV campgrounds are set up for service in this position.

If you build in components, for example a water tank under the counter, be sure to make provisions for its repair or removal without tearing the counter apart. RV manufacturers typically install these features so that the water tank can be removed through the opening created when the stove is removed. Likewise, be sure that the water lines and plumbing have repair access.

Suggested Conversion Sequence

1. Level the bus. The bus floor MUST be level so the walls will be plumb and the counters and refrigerator will be level during use.

2. Install the plywood subfloor using at least ½" plywood.

3. Install framing for any walls, closets, cabinets, counters, and built-in appliances. **NOTE: You should bolt or screw and glue everything possible. If it isn't properly secured now, it will probably squeak and creek later.**

4. Install plumbing, wiring, and LP gas lines as needed through the framing and floor. Be sure to cap off all lines to prevent foreign materials from entering the system. NOTE: Be sure to pad LP gas lines and electrical wiring to protect against chaffing. Pay special attention to areas where they pass through the floor. **These lines MUST NOT touch the metal as chaffing will promote wearing of the lines and wiring with obvious results.** You can make these pads yourself with a strip of old tire side wall or purchase specially designed grommets from larger hardware, electrical or automotive accessory stores.

5. Install below bus plumbing, wiring, LP gas lines, cabinets, holding tanks, etc. Be sure that holding tanks and cabinets do not block access to plumbing and LP gas connections. Also, install a **low point drain valve** so the water system can be drained for winterization.

6. Install paneling, cabinets and accessories. Ensure that all electrical accessories are properly grounded. As you install appliances, try to leave as much maintenance space as practical. Check each component and system as you go. The few minutes you invest now can save you many hours later.

7. Install the refrigerator. It is vital that the floor is level first, and then level the refrigerator in the bus. While not as critical, this also goes for countertops. You should also obtain a "bulls eye" level for checking level at the campsite. They are small, inexpensive, and a good investment. You can use a jack and some blocks to level the bus if necessary. Failure to have a level refrigerator could result, as we learned the hard way, in your refrigerator becoming a hot box. Newer RV refrigerators aren't quite so level critical, but will be more efficient (and you'll be more comfortable) if the floor is level.

8. Paint, carpet, tile, etc. as desired.

9. When you install delicate electronics equipment, keep in mind that there is a great deal of shock movement, especially in the rear of the bus. Radios, TVs, microwave ovens, etc. should be shock mounted or padded for protection against vibration.

8. Raising the Roof

Warning: This project is not for the novice. Buses are designed to withstand the effects of a simple roll over accident. Unless a roof raise is carefully engineered and properly completed, the structural integrity is at risk putting you and your passengers in grave peril.

Raising the roof involves disconnecting and raising all (or a portion of) the roof, inserting rib spacers, reattaching the roof, adding new sheet metal, reconfiguring the windows and blending the new roofline with the coach while trying for a professional appearance. In addition to adding a feeling of more room, the completed project effects structural integrity, watertight integrity, clearance and your pocket book.

> ~WARNING~
> Raising the roof is an expensive, dangerous and difficult project. You are risking personal injury as well as the structural integrity of the coach.

Careful planning and engineering are essential to achieving a safe, secure, watertight and esthetically pleasing finished project.

Once the decision is made to raise the roof,

a number of options must be considered:

- ❑ How much to raise the roof
- ❑ Whether to raise all or a portion of the roof
- ❑ Whether to buy special RV windows or reuse the existing coach windows
- ❑ Make sure your new roofline will not exceed maximum vehicle height.

How much should you raise the roof?
Many commercial RVs have a 6'6" ceiling height. This generally provides sufficient clearance for lighting, roof mounted air conditioners and other accessories. However, a bus may require more centerline clearance to compensate for the curvature of the bus roof.

The more you raise the roof the more difficult it will be to blend the raised section in with the rest of the roofline. Also, extreme changes will have a greater effect on structural integrity than modest changes.

Another factor is, every inch you raise the roof of a 30-foot bus increases interior volume by about 19 cubic feet. A 6-inch rise will give you an additional 110-115 cubic feet to heat or air condition.

Be sure to take planned floor and ceiling treatments into account. A headliner plus a new layer of plywood and carpeting on the floor will take at least 1" to 1 ½".

Should you raise all or a portion of the roof? Some converters separate the entire roof, starting just above the windshield and ending where the roof meets the back door frame. While this will give you a more symmetrical, uniform appearance, it is

probably more difficult than a partial roof raise. It often requires difficult modifications to the windshield mounting, rear door mounting and the entry door. The Blackman's chose this method. Their website has excellent detailed information and photos.
http://busweb.freeservers.com/busweb.htm

Another option is a partial roof raise. The roof is cut aft of the front cap, and the rear cap is disconnected from the back. With this method, the windshield and its framing are undisturbed, and almost the entire roof is raised. The front cap and raised portion can then be blended in with a "step-up" appearance and there is only one seam on the roof to reconnect, seal and taper.

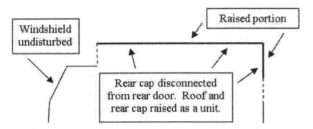

Windows. If you plan to Reuse the existing bus windows you can often do so by simply adding spacers to the top and/or bottom of the newly enlarged opening and reinstalling them. Replacing them with new RV windows will involve modifying the placement of the vertical ribs and will affect structural integrity.

Suggested sequence. Important note: These guidelines are generic. **Every bus is different and you *will* have to modify the sequence and methods to suit your particular situation.**

Remove the windows. This can usually be accomplished by removing a few mounting screws or rivets and prying them out.

Lifting mechanism. There are a number

of lifting choices available. The Blackmans used a system of camper jacks and clamps. (See their website, listed earlier in this chapter, for photos and details.)

Another method is described on the following pages. It involves a come-along at each of 4 corners of a framework.

Prepare a framework. This will be used to lift the roof, provide vertical, forward/aft and lateral stability and facilitate the reinstallation. The framework will be most stable if it is mounted flush with the sides of the bus. The bus itself will act as a brace of sorts. Be sure to check clearance between the roof and the supports. You may have to shim the supports slightly from the bus sides so the

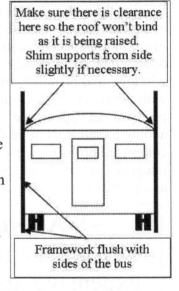

roof can be raised without binding. Clamp the vertical supports to the sides of the bus to prevent movement.

If you are going to raise the entire roof, remove front entry door and loosen the front and rear caps while leaving the casing around the rear door and windshield intact, if possible. For safety, the windshield should be removed and stored to prevent accidental breakage.

If you are not disconnecting the front cap, remove the entry door and make your lateral cuts just aft of the front cap. A skill saw with a metal blade works well but keep

- **DO NOT make any cuts with the roof unsupported!** Cut the inside layer of skin first, then move outside. If your support mechanism fails it would be better to fall on the roof than have it fall on you!

- **Always wear eye protection.**

- **Keep your hands, and anything else you would like to keep, away from the edges of the cut.** The edges will be extremely sharp and the roof is likely to shift as the cut is completed, providing an efficient impromptu amputation device!

- **Never work alone** when doing this type of work. As a minimum, have a safety observer with a phone handy in case of accident. (Your teenage son or daughter with a set of headphones and a CD player is probably *not* your best candidate for a safety observer.)

the cut shallow. If your bus has insulation in the roof, a deep cut will clog the blade.

Watch out for electrical wiring which will be present for bus lights and accessories. Some buses may also have ducting in the ceiling.

You will need a jigsaw for the ceiling in the corners where curvature is most pronounced.

Try to stay away from the joints in the roof and ceiling when planning your lateral cuts. These are extremely difficult to cut.

Apply <u>slight</u> upward pressure to the roof; with the come alongs, just enough to keep the roof from dropping as the ribs are cut.

Recheck tension after cutting each pair of ribs.

Use a circular saw with a metal cutting blade for cutting ribs. Do not use a cutting torch. A cutting torch will leave ragged, uneven ribs. You will need clean, uniform cuts to weld the extensions.

You can construct a simple guide to ensure a uniform 90° cut using a couple of 10-foot 1" x 4"s (one for each side of the bus) and some clamps. Simply clamp the 1" x 4" to the ribs at 90° and rest the saw on the 1" x 4" as you cut. As you finish a section of ribs, move the guide rearward for the next set. See illustration 8-c on Page 8-4.

Check and adjust the vertical tension frequently using the comealongs at each corner, to prevent the blade from binding as you move from rib to rib.

Be sure to stagger your cuts, DO NOT cut all ribs in the same location. This will create a weak junction or a natural "hinge" that could fail easily in an accident. A 6" spacer will raise the roof 6" regardless of its position in the rib. To make installation of spacers easier, void making the cut at either the top or bottom of the rib. It would make it more difficult to weld the spacer in place.

Starting at the front of the bus, cut the first vertical rib at an exact 90° angle. Move to the opposite side of the bus and cut the corresponding rib.

Work aft, cutting ribs in pairs with the skill saw until all ribs are cut. Once again, check and adjust the upward pressure on the roof as necessary after each set of cuts, applying *just enough pressure to keep the blade from binding as a rib is cut.*

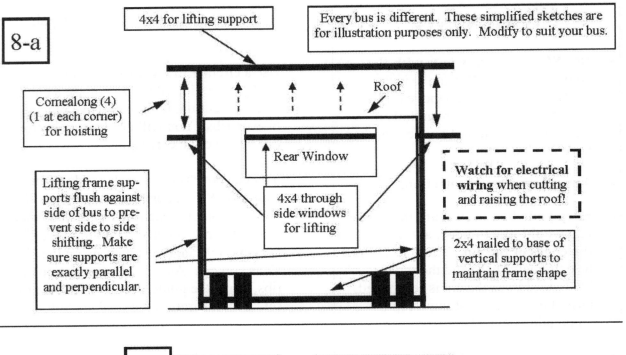

8-a

4x4 for lifting support

Every bus is different. These simplified sketches are for illustration purposes only. Modify to suit your bus.

Comealong (4) (1 at each corner) for hoisting

Roof

Rear Window

Lifting frame supports flush against side of bus to prevent side to side shifting. Make sure supports are exactly parallel and perpendicular.

4x4 through side windows for lifting

Watch for electrical wiring when cutting and raising the roof!

2x4 nailed to base of vertical supports to maintain frame shape

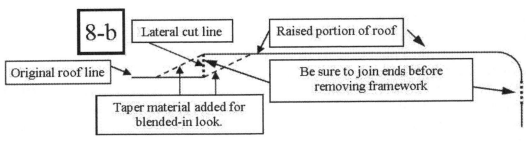

8-b

Lateral cut line

Raised portion of roof

Original roof line

Be sure to join ends before removing framework

Taper material added for blended-in look.

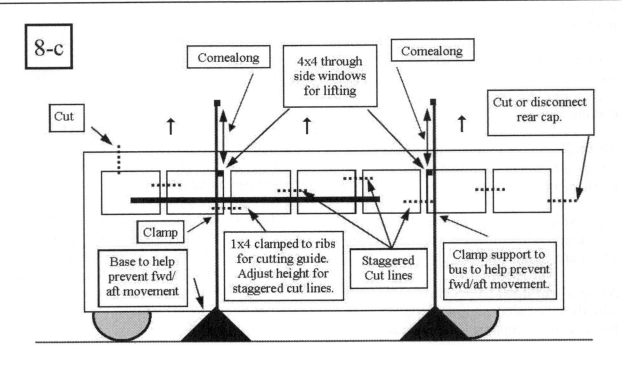

8-c

Comealong

4x4 through side windows for lifting

Comealong

Cut

Cut or disconnect rear cap.

Clamp

1x4 clamped to ribs for cutting guide. Adjust height for staggered cut lines.

Staggered Cut lines

Clamp support to bus to help prevent fwd/aft movement.

Base to help prevent fwd/ aft movement

After all ribs are cut, uniformly raise the roof just enough to install the spacers. Be careful to avoid forward/aft and lateral movement of the roof; the lift must be as near perfectly vertical as possible. This is why it is important that the lift supports be clamped to the sides of the bus.

As you raise the roof, watch for wiring in the ceiling at both ends. If you are leaving existing lights in place, carefully cut the wires and tie a string to the ends so they don't get pulled back into the roof cavity.

If you are raising the entire roof, special attention must be paid to the windshield to prevent damage.

Some converters cut out and discard a small section (about one foot) of the roof at one or both ends to facilitate tapering the ends of the roofline and ceiling. **This is NOT recommended as it makes securing the ends much more difficult and increases the risk of failure.**

Rib spacers. Simple flat iron is NOT recommended. Try to match the original rib contour if possible or use square tubing or similar material for spacers. Each bus is different, so use the best material for your application. *Be sure that all spacers are cut square and are of identical length.*

Rib spacer installation. Once again, starting at the front, weld the first set of spacers to the cut ribs of the bus body and roof, being careful to ensure no forward/aft or lateral movement has occurred. Work aft, welding ribs in pairs, easing upward tension to the roof as necessary to ensure correct mating of the ribs and spacers.

After all ribs have been reconnected and **before removing the lifting framework** or fully releasing upward tension, **join the cut**

ends of the roof together so lateral movement is not possible.

The roof will not be stable until this step is completed. A stiff wind has the potential of causing the roof to collapse on the ribs.

Join before removing supports.

This is also a good time to install and/or reconnect wiring for roof mounted air conditioners, lights and other accessories.

Once roof ends have been properly joined at <u>both</u> ends, the framework may be removed. The structure will not be fully stable, however, until new sheet metal is installed.

Below: Ribs cut and roof raised X inches. Be sure to stagger the cuts as shown to avoid a weak point in the structure. A 6" spacer inserted anywhere in a rib will raise the roof 6" regardless of its position.

This drawing represents ribs cut and spacers of identical lengths ready to be welded into place. Inserts should be at least equal in strength to the original material.

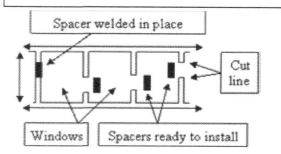

25

9. Making Contour Layouts

The drawings and text (edited) in this section are from *How To Build Low Cost Motorhomes* by Louis C. McClure, Copyright© 1973 by Louis C. McClure, and used with his kind permission.

Note: If you plan to raise the roof, make your contour layout *after* the roof raise is completed. (Duh!)

It is essential that partitions and cabinets fit the sidewalls and ceiling of the coach properly. Poor fits are the hallmark of an amateur. One of the biggest problems the converter faces is making an accurate pattern for the sidewall and ceiling of the bus to assist in achieving a professional appearance.

There is no such animal as a "standard" contour for bus sidewalls and ceilings, except for within the same make and model. Even then, you will encounter small variations. So, you are left to your own devices to create a useable pattern.

There are two methods. The first, and simplest, is by taking a large sheet of cardboard and trimming the edges as required, by trial and error, to conform to the contour of the wall and ceiling.

A more scientific approach is to use a Contour Layout Board.

Making the Contour Layout Board

Figure 9-a. Cut a 1" x 6" to the exact width of the inside of the bus, at a point at or near the junction of the ceiling and sidewall. The top of the window on each side usually has a small ledge on which the board can be placed and is a good reference point in many cases. Because of the taper of the wall at this point, you will have to trim the ends to make it fit correctly.

Using screws, attach a 1" x 4" to each end of the 1" x 6" at a right angle, extending to the floor. If the 1" x 6" is properly positioned, the lengths of both 1" x 4"'s should be identical. If not, make the necessary adjustment before proceeding.

Cut a 1" x 2" (shown in

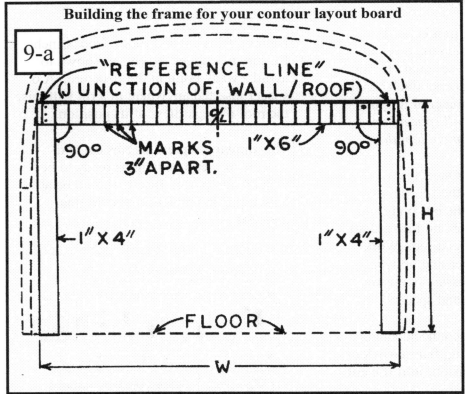

Building the frame for your contour layout board

9-a

"REFERENCE LINE"
(JUNCTION OF WALL/ROOF)

90°   MARKS   1"X6"   90°
3"APART.

1"X4"   1"X4"

H

FLOOR

W

Figure 9-c) the same length as the 1" x 6" and attach it to the bottom of the 1" x 4"s with screws, completing the rectangle.

In many buses the sides are cambered, sloped or curved. If so, ensure that the distance between the base of each "leg" and the wall is identical. Secure your frame in place to prevent shifting while making and recording measurements.

Figure 9-b. Next, locate the exact lateral center on the 1" x 6". Using a tri-square or combination machinist's square, scribe a line at this point and label it "Centerline".

Beginning at the centerline, working toward each side, use your square and scribe 90° lines across the 1" x 6" at 3" intervals. When within one foot of each side where the curvature of the ceiling becomes more pronounced, place the lines closer together, approximately 1 ½ inches apart.

Using a long ruler or yardstick, measure the vertical distance from the top edge of the 1" x 6" to the ceiling at each scribe mark. Make sure the yardstick or ruler is accurately aligned with the scribe mark before making the measurement. Indicate the exact measurement on the 1" x 6" for each scribe mark.

Locate the points of separation between the sidewall of the bus and the outer edges of the 1" x 4". Measure this separation and indicate the measurement on the 1" x 4"s on each side as shown. When you are done, cross measure the structure by measuring and recording the distance

diagonally between the outside bottom left leg and the outside upper right corner of the 1" x 6".

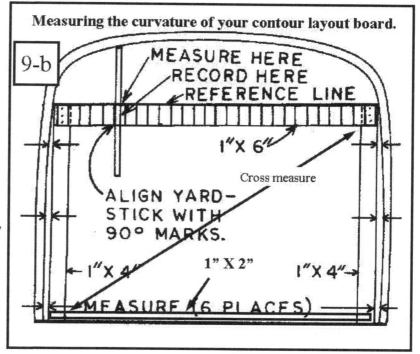

Measuring the curvature of your contour layout board.

Figure 9-c. You might be able to remove the contour layout frame from the bus intact. If not, carefully disassemble it and reassemble the pattern upon two side-by-side sheets of ½" plywood. Ensure the centerline of the 1" x 6" is located at the junction of the two sheets. The 1" x 2" should be flush with the "bottom" of the panels. Verify the cross measurement you made to ensure the structure retains its true shape. Any adjustments need to be made now.

Due to irregularities in bus bodies, especially older models, it is possible that the center lines on both the 1" x 6" and the 1" x 2" won't line up with the junction of the two sheets of plywood when the cross measurement is verified. In this case, ensure that the 1" x 6" is aligned with the junction and the cross measurement should prevail. If everything looks right, temporarily tack the frame to the plywood to prevent shifting.

This is not a time to be in a hurry. If your measurements are off or the frame is not correctly positioned, the pattern will be inaccurate resulting in misfitting walls and cabinets, so double check your measurements.

It is now time to reproduce the curvature of your bus in a useable form. Again, accurately align the yardstick or ruler with each scribe mark on the 1" x 6" and measure up the distance indicated, placing a dot on the plywood. Follow the same procedure with the 1" x 4"s to reconstruct the sidewall curvature.

Now all you have to do is "connect the dots" for an accurate, full-scale contour layout for your bus!

Before you remove the frame and cut out the panels, you might want to draw a horizontal line on the panels along the top of the 1" x 6", and a similar parallel line about every 6" or so to give you reference lines for constructing overhead cabinets.

Be sure to label the patterns "Left" and "Right".

Finally, "cut on the dotted lines" and you will have a full-scale template of the cross-section of your bus. This will become your master pattern during the construction of wardrobes,

bathroom walls and partitions, cabinets, etc. When completed, the patterns themselves may be used as partitions if desired.

It will likely be necessary to "trim" panels slightly to ensure perfect fit at any particular point. Bus bodies often vary as much as plus or minus ¼ inch throughout the unit. Trimming may be accomplished by use of a block plane, rasp, or sander.

When installing partitions and cabinets, recommend that you install appropriate vinyl molding between the partition or cabinet and the sidewall or ceiling. This vinyl molding is available at trailer supply stores and effectively hides minor misfits.

Cutting out your pattern

DOTS — CUT ON LINE — 9-c

Verify cross measurement

ALIGN YARD-STICK WITH 90° MARKS.

4' X 8' X 1/2"   4' X 8' X 1/2"
PLYWOOD   PLYWOOD
1" X 2"

10. Solar Energy

They say that "You can't take it with you." But in the case of electric power, that is no big deal. If you have the proper equipment, all the electrical power you will need for long term RVing in the outback is already there, just waiting for you to tap in.

No, we're not talking about anything illegal, just an unlimited source of free electrical power.

While your refrigerator, water heater, range and other energy magnets remain more economical to operate using LPG, for as little as about $500.00, you can be truly self contained and independent. A simple one panel solar system will power your lights and water pump, even a small TV indefinitely.

And since solar systems are easily expandable, you can add more solar panels later to carry heavier loads like microwave ovens, toasters, VCRs and the other modern creature comforts.

The RV air conditioner, on the other hand, uses so much power it cannot be run with any but the most elaborate (expensive) systems.

Solar energy systems are not for everyone. The campers who spend the majority of their vacation in an RV park with only brief stops in remote locations, could probably do quite well with just the house battery or a small generator. For the heartier soul, a solar system can make long outback stays much more enjoyable.

How solar electric equipment works in your RV

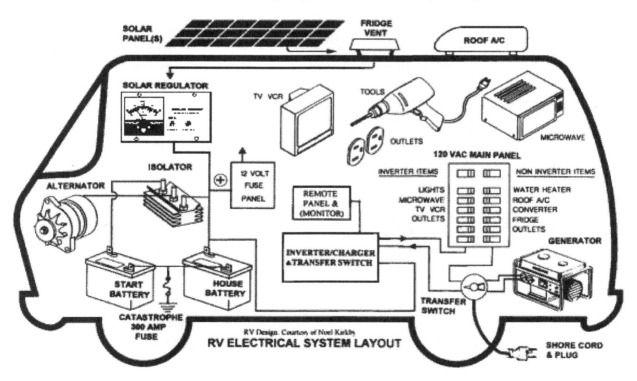

RV Design: Courtesy of Noel Kirby
RV ELECTRICAL SYSTEM LAYOUT

The primary purpose of the solar system is to recharge batteries without starting the generator or plugging into power. Nearly all solar systems consist of four basic components: Solar panel(s), a charge controller, mounting structure and a wiring harness

While a solar system can be used to simply recharge batteries, it can also be expanded and used in conjunction with an inverter which converts the battery's DC power to usable AC power for your appliances.

The typical RVer using 12 volt items like fans & lights along with an inverter to power a microwave and toaster would need a system consisting of two panels of approximately 75-120 watts each and an inverter with 1500-2000 watts capacity

Complete solar and inverter systems in this range cost approximately $2200-2700 depending on the components used.

Although this may seem like a high upfront cost, the system requires no other maintenance and has a service life of 20+ years, making it more affordable than it would seem at first glance.

If you like adventure and have little use for the beaten path, a solar system might be worth a closer look. In addition to a fact-filled, user friendly website, RV Solar Electric, Inc. has complete kits and guides to help make the transition to energy independence as smooth as possible.

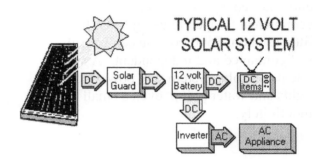

TYPICAL 12 VOLT SOLAR SYSTEM

Sample table used to calculate energy usage for solar design.
This sample would require only one solar panel.

Item	Amps	x Hr/day =	AH/day
15 watt fluorescent light	1.0	6.0	6.0
Two 12v incandescent lamp	1.5	2.0	6.0
TV (9" color) 12 volt	3.0	4.0	12.0
Water pump (12 min/day)	8.0	0.2 (12/60=.2 hr)	1.6
12 volt stereo	0.8	2.0	1.6
		Total AH used per day =	27.2

Artwork and tables are courtesy of Doug Kirkby, RV Solar Electric, Inc.

sunshine into electricity

RV Solar Electric Inc.
14415 N. 73rd Street
Scottsdale, AZ 85260

http://www.rvsolarelectric.com/
E-mail: rvse@mindspring.com
Phone: 1-800-999-8520

11. Safety and Security

You are going to be working with electricity, explosives (gasoline and LPG), power tools, heavy parts and appliances and other dangerous items. Work with a partner if you can and use extreme caution.

Be sure to get your bus **title** nomenclature changed to "Housecar", "Motorhome" or whatever your state calls it.

You may want to have higher **insurance** coverage for your bus than on your car. A bus weighing several tons can do a great deal more damage than a 2000-lb. car.

> <u>IMPORTANT</u>: **Insurance for home conversions, especially school bus conversions, is becoming increasingly more difficult to obtain.**
> **They are considered high risk.**

If your insurance company does not offer coverage, try National General Insurance Company at (800) 847-2886.

Before construction, obtain a copy of your states **building codes for RVs**. Your RV dealer should know if your state has an RV building code and how you can obtain a copy.

If your state does not have its own code, the National Fire Protection Association publishes *NFPA 1192: Standard on Recreational Vehicles*. The book can be

ordered from Amazon. COM. A direct link to this book is available at **httw://www.rv-busconversions.com/books**

In some states you may have difficulty selling your coach and you may be turned away from some RV parks if it doesn't meet these standards.

Electricity

Be sure that your AC accessories are properly grounded and are correctly connected with circuit breakers! Remember that your coach is made of steel, an excellent conductor of electricity. **You should consider having your electrical systems safety checked by a qualified electrician.**

LPG (Propane)

Mount your LP gas tanks *above* bumper level in case of accident or use special tanks that mount under the coach.

Each gas accessory should have it's own **gas shutoff** so it can be isolated in case of partial LP gas system failure.

Test each connection with a soap solution *not* a match. The Darwin Awards come to mind. **http://www.darwinawards.com/**

Ensure that all gas appliances have proper **ventilation** and exhaust flow. This is another area where it might be a good idea to get professional help.

Use approved **fire resistant material** and maintain recommended clearances around the range, furnace refrigerator and water heater.

Install a **smoke/fire detector** and a **gas pollution alarm**. The gas pollution alarm detects the presence of toxic gasses. Several models are available. See your RV accessory dealer for applications.

Be careful in the placement of **curtains** around the range and other gas appliances.

Water

It seems that Mexico is not the only place that Montezuma had his revenge. Be sure  to sample or test the **drinking water** while on the road BEFORE filling your tanks. Some RV owners also install water filtration systems.

Be sure to connect a **pressure regulator** to the **water supply** before connecting the hose. Some RV parks have extremely high water pressure and you risk your hose and the coach's plumbing. This $10.00 item could save you hundreds of dollars in repairs.

Holding Tank

Ensure that the holding tank is **vented** to eliminate the build-up of explosive and unpleasant "natural gas" (methane.) The holding tank is vented through the roof.

Ensure that all drains are connected to **traps**.

Locks

Install a hasp on the rear door so you can lock the bus when you leave. Also install an **extra** eye so the hasp can be **locked** in the **open** position. This might prevent someone from accidentally locking you in

the bus, creating a potential death trap if there should be a fire or gas leak. See illustration on Page 45. A garage door lock, available at the hardware store, would also be suitable.

Install a bar lock (one of the free things we discussed earlier) on the front and rear doors. See Page 46.

The driver's side window is often the sliding type without a lock. After all, who would want to break into a bus? Install a lock! A lock designed for sliding windows is available at most hardware stores.

General Safety Tips

Install **catches** on all drawers, cupboards and cabinet doors.

Install **coat hooks** and like items *above* eye level.

Install and use **seat belts**.

 **Avoid cooking** while on the road. An emergency stop or other quick maneuver could result in being scalded, increasing the possibility of a serious accident.

Ensure that everything in the coach is secure. Coffee cups, frying pans, peppershakers, towels, and anything else loose is a potential missile or blindfold.

Safety Supplies

As a **minimum**, carry an approved fire extinguisher, a first aid kit, and a supply of flares or reflective markers.

Gasoline Safety

One of the most dangerous commodities we own is gasoline. We use it daily in our cars, lawn mowers and boats. We store it carelessly in sheds, in our car's trunk; we clean paint brushes and car parts with it. We take it for granted.

Paul's father is a veteran mechanic with 50 years experience. He taught his son about the dangers of gasoline and safety precautions to take while working with it. Monday, Paul skipped a step. Instead of filling the tank with water to purge the fumes, he merely drained it and vented the tank for 24 hours. This was not enough.

While removing the tank, bare metal rubbing against bare metal produced a spark. The spark ignited the fumes, sending a fireball into the air that left Paul's shirt melted to his chest and painful burns on his head and chest. Fortunately, his injuries are relatively minor. After all, gas tank explosions have been known to rip an automobile in half. He could easily have been killed or blinded. Paul will heal, but I doubt that he will soon forget.

Paul (yes, that's his real name) asked me to share this experience and some safety tips to use when working with gas tanks in the hopes of preventing this from happening to you.

- Work with a partner for safety in case of accident or fire and have a fire extinguisher handy.
- Work in a safe area with no open flames or smoking.
- Ensure that the propane is turned off and all appliances are cold. Check the pilot lights!
- Disconnect and remove all batteries and electrical power sources from the vehicle.
- Disconnect all wiring to the tank (i.e. sending unit, internal fuel pump) EXCEPT the ground wire. USE BRASS TOOLS IF POSSIBLE to reduce the possibility of sparking.
- Disconnect the fuel line and plug it. Then drain the tank.
- Fill the tank with water to purge all the fumes. An "empty" gas tank containing "nothing more than fumes" is far more volatile than a full one.
- After all fumes have dissipated, drain the tank and remove the ground strap.
- Hose down the tank and cavity to reduce sparking and remove the tank.

Paul, a few days before the accident

4. 3. 2001

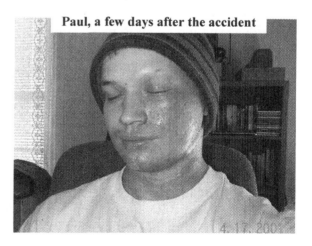

Paul, a few days after the accident

4. 17. 2001

Thank you, Paul, for your courage in sharing your painful experience with us.

12. Basic Floor Plans

I have been asked about plans for a typical bus conversion. Unfortunately, there is no such animal. There are simply too many variables such as length, curvature of the walls/roof, location of engine and bus accessories, floor configurations, cargo bays and ceiling height, just to name a few. Unless you are converting a fleet of the same make and model coach, you pretty much have to start from scratch and play it by ear.

The first four drawings are the simplest of the simple and are provided to give you ideas for brainstorming your own design.

Feel free to mix and match. You may like some of the ideas presented in one plan, some of another. Be creative. Use your own ideas and judgment to make your bus the way you want it.

As was mentioned earlier in the text, when making your plans, don't forget to check *under* the bus to ensure that plumbing or other features you want to install will not interfere with bus parts and accessories.

It is a good idea to look at several commercially built RVs when considering a floor plan. RV manufacturers are experts in economizing on space and you will pick

up a few pointers.

For short buses try to obtain a two-burner gas stove, single bowl sink, and gas refrigerator in one unit. They may still be available, but you may have to special order it through LP appliance or RV Dealers.

Other options you might consider include a convertible **RV dinette** set which doubles as a bed, instead of bus seats and a table. You can either buy these units or make them yourself.

You might choose a **standard bed** or sofa bed instead of bunks. I have even seen a waterbed in the rear of a long bus.

While this may sound like a great idea, I feel it would be dangerous. A waterbed is extremely heavy and would be unstable in a moving bus. Inertia is a powerful force. An emergency stop or accident could cause the entire waterbed mattress to "flow" out of its frame and it could crush anything (or anyone) in its path.

Cornering and handling would also be affected, not to mention the excess weight, resulting in overstress of suspension parts.

Reading the sample floor plans

You will note that 3 of the 4 sample floor plans use a shower and commode in one small area. This same system is employed on many commercially built RVs.

From an overhead viewpoint, the center section, outlined by heavy lines, is the floor. The section to the left and right are the view of the left and right sides of the bus, respectively, which have been laid flat.

The top of the page is the front; the lower part of the page is the rear of the bus.

You will notice that the floor plans start behind the driver's area, or at the "White line." Please note that all corners are squared for ease in illustration although they will be rounded in the bus.

Windows have not been drawn on any illustrations and overhead cupboards were only drawn on the illustration on Page 38 in order to simplify the drawings. You can easily adapt the same cupboard ideas to all floor plans.

The long bus used in my illustration had a 25' floor length as measured from the "while line". The short bus had 14' and, as today's auto dealers are prone to say, "Use these figures for comparison, yours may vary."

When planning your bus floor plan, you might want to consider the **Floor Planner Kit.** The kit includes a 30" x 48" sheet of ¼" gridded vellum and special Col-Erase pencils. Vellum is a 100% cotton media and was designed for professional draftsmen. With the kit you can plan a 45' bus with 1"=1' scale with room for both side elevations. The kit is available from http://www.rv-busconversions.com/

Key

Use the following as your key for the first four plans:

B-l   Bunk
B-2   Bunk – see illustration on Page 44.
C   Commode
D   Dinette
E   Entertainment area (TV, Radio, etc.)
F   Furnace
R   Range, with or without oven
R-8   Refrigerator/Ice box. (Number indicates approximate maximum cubic feet)
S   Sink
SB-l   Sofa bed (back folds down)
SB-2   Standard foldout sofa bed.
SH   Shower
X   Suggested light locations

Sample floor plan #1. 14-foot four sleeper

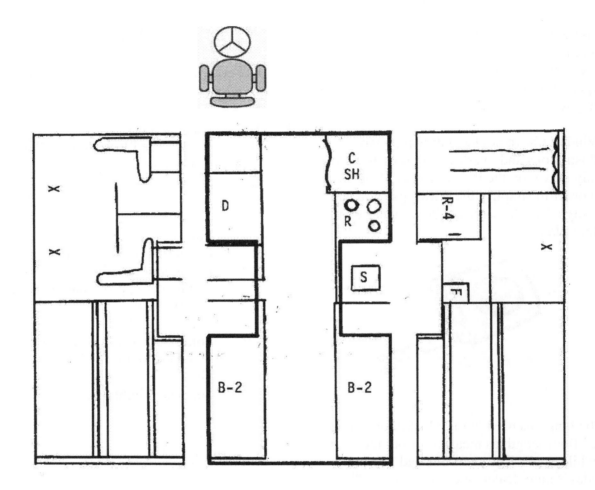

Sample floor plan 1 is designed for four persons and has the smallest living area and kitchen of any bus shown. Note that the range is directly over the refrigerator and that this design features no oven, although an overhead model could be installed.

It utilizes special bunks (Page 44) with the base of the bottom bunks somewhat deeper and shorter to fit in with the wheel wells.

No closets are included.

Sample floor plan #2. 14-foot two sleeper

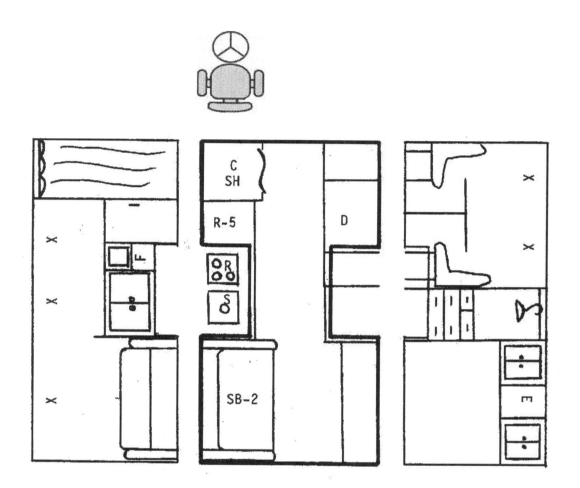

This design would work well for a couple.

It features a standard sofa bed, entertainment area, half closet/dresser combination and an adequate kitchen.

Note that the entertainment area is located rather high. When the sofa bed is folded out, the end will be directly below it.

Sample floor plan #3. 25-foot 6 sleeper with bunks

Driver

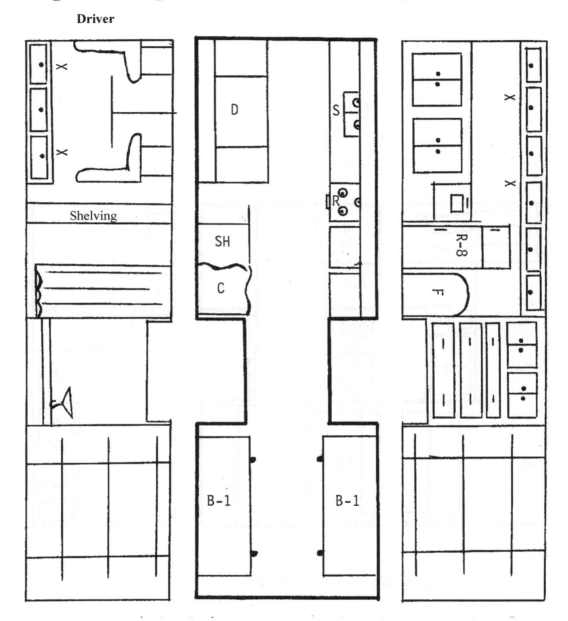

Shelving

D

S

SH

C

R

R-8

F

B-1

B-1

This plan features a large bathroom, centralized furnace, and 8 cubic foot freestanding refrigerator, double sink and ample counter space.

Shelves behind the dinette face forward and are a good place for towels and linens. Be sure to have a front piece on the cabinet to prevent items from flying out during a stop or, as an alternative, make a pull-out pantry.

Our first sKOOLie looked much like this except that we used a sofa bed and entertainment center instead of bunks. The plan worked very well for the two of us.

Sample floor plan #4. 25-foot 6 sleeper

Driver

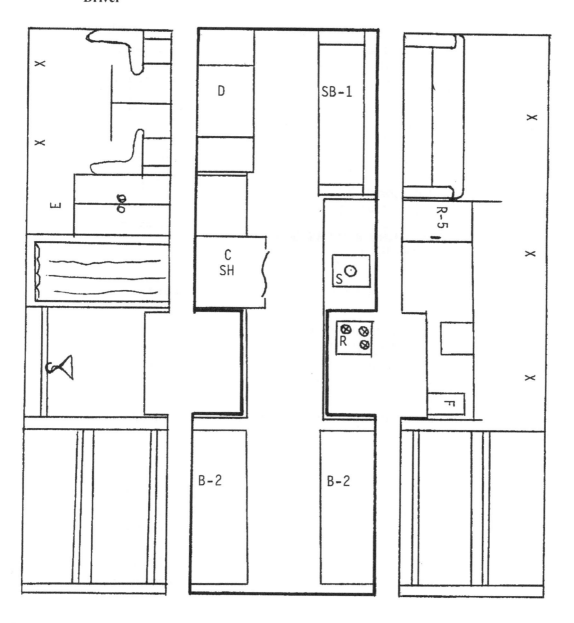

Special bunks (Page 44) eliminate the need for a dresser. The commode and shower are located in the same space, like many of today's professionally built RVs.

This design allows for more counter space than the other designs, due to smaller, built-in refrigerator.

The convertible dinette and sofa provide the 5th and 6th beds.

35-foot Youth group mission bus

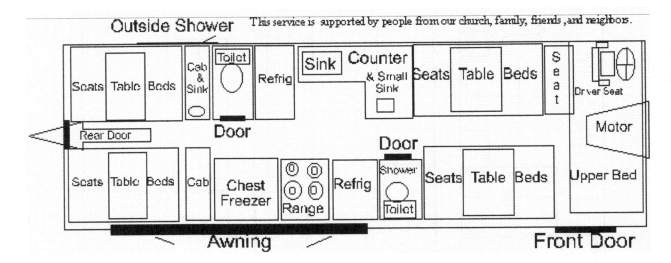

"Wherever God Wills - Donde Dios Quiera"

A former Army bus, this 1983 International Harvester was converted by a Christian youth group support service in Grand Rapids, MI as a mobile platform from which to perform service projects. With careful planning and engineering, they have packed more features into this 35-foot bus than most people have in their homes.

Designed to accommodate a twelve-member youth group, two adult leaders, a driver and a cook, the bus features:

- 6000 watt generator
- 4 dinettes (convert to beds)
- 4 bunks (over dinettes)
- 2-30 amp converters
- 20 gallon water heater
- 2-18 cu. ft. refrigerators

- 9 cu. ft. chest freezer
- 140 gallon fresh water tank
- 2 bathrooms (1 with shower)
- 30" LP gas range
- RV (vented) LPG heater
- 5 roof vent/escape hatches

The Blickleys have been assisting youth groups and providing bus lodging/transportation for projects since 1993. For more information on their bus conversion and their work, visit their web site at: **http://www.wherevergodwills.org/**.

Courtesy: Bill and LaVerne Blickley

Joreth's International sKOOLie featured on Page 50.

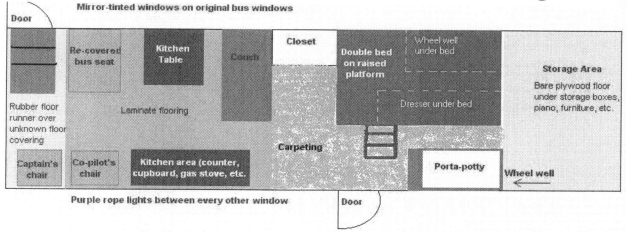

Tony Basely's coach is featured on Page 52.

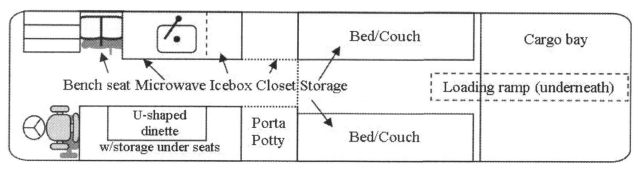

Jim Sims' coach is featured on Page 76.

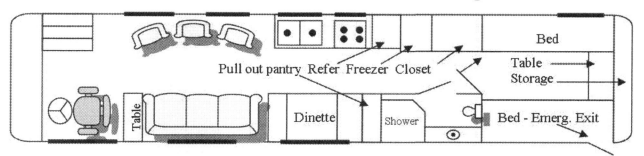

"Cal" McClure's Gillig is featured on Page 78.

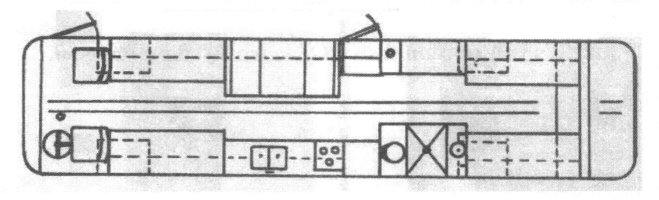

The "DAFfy Canuck" is featured on page 81.

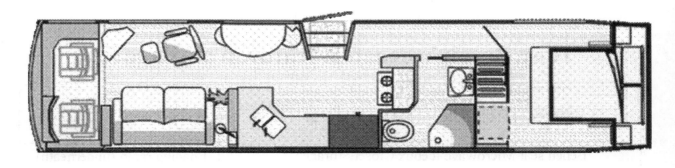

"Grace" is featured on Page 85.

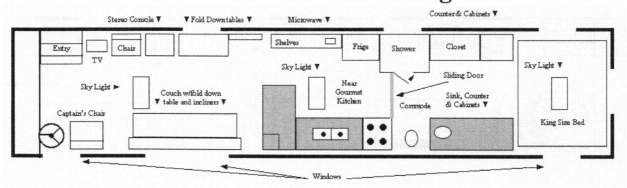

RETALES

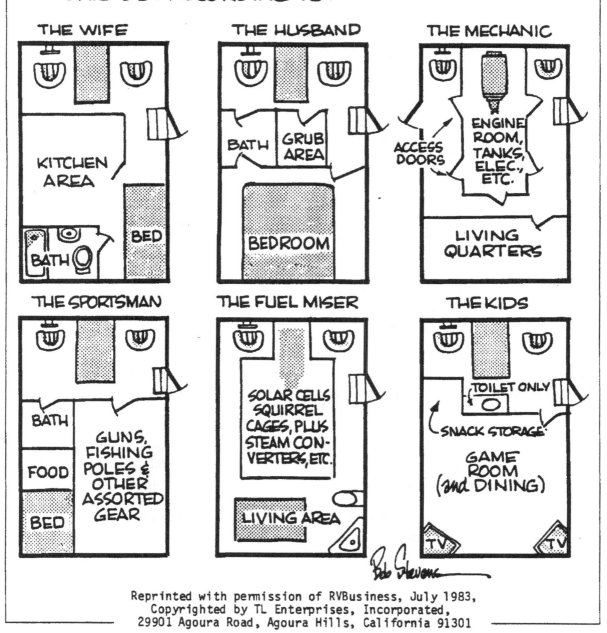

WHAT DO RVers REALLY WANT IN A FLOOR-PLAN? NEEDS VARY. WE PRESENT HERE AN RV WITH THE SAME OUTSIDE DIMENSIONS BUT LAID OUT ACCORDING TO:

THE WIFE

KITCHEN AREA

BATH

BED

THE HUSBAND

BATH · GRUB AREA

BEDROOM

THE MECHANIC

ACCESS DOORS

ENGINE ROOM, TANKS, ELEC., ETC.

LIVING QUARTERS

THE SPORTSMAN

BATH

FOOD

BED

GUNS, FISHING POLES & OTHER ASSORTED GEAR

THE FUEL MISER

SOLAR CELLS SQUIRREL CAGES, PLUS STEAM CONVERTERS, ETC.

LIVING AREA

THE KIDS

TOILET ONLY

SNACK STORAGE

GAME ROOM (and DINING)

TV   TV

Reprinted with permission of RVBusiness, July 1983,
Copyrighted by TL Enterprises, Incorporated,
29901 Agoura Road, Agoura Hills, California 91301

13. Illustrations
Bunk with built-in storage

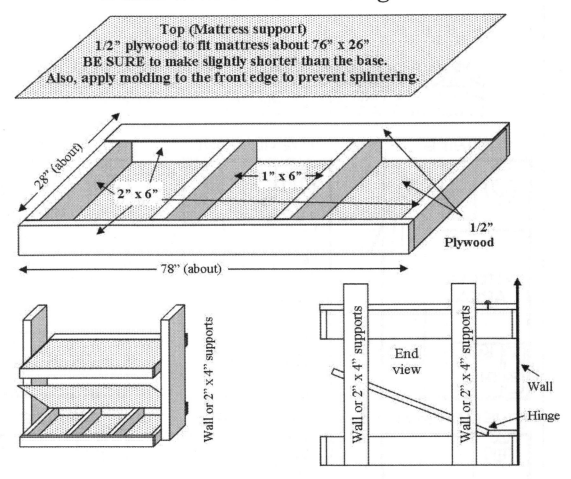

Top (Mattress support)
1/2" plywood to fit mattress about 76" x 26"
BE SURE to make slightly shorter than the base.
Also, apply molding to the front edge to prevent splintering.

28" (about)

2" x 6"

1" x 6"

1/2" Plywood

78" (about)

Wall or 2" x 4" supports

Wall or 2" x 4" supports

End view

Wall or 2" x 4" supports

Wall

Hinge

This type of bunk eliminates the need for a dresser and is quite common aboard ship in the Navy. It is made of two parts: the base, sort of a long, flat box, and the top that supports the mattress. The top is hinged at the back to allow access to the clothes below.

Mount the bases in first, set the tops on the bases and attach to the base with hinges as shown. Be sure to make the top slightly shorter than the base to eliminate binding on the wall or support posts. You can add privacy curtains and reading lights as desired.

The short section of plywood on the base (best seen in the end view) allows the top to be raised without compressing the mattress.

The support posts are secured to both the floor and the ceiling and the bunk's base can be attached directly to the wall.

Add a 4" or 6" foam mattress for a firm, yet comfortable bed.

44

Extra Eye feature for your rear door lock

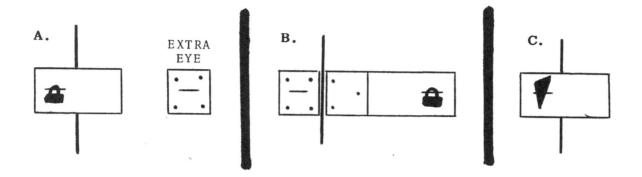

A. Rear door locked from the outside. The front door should also be locked from the inside.
B. Rear door locked in the "open" position using the Extra Eye. The door can still be locked from the inside using the Free Bar Lock. (Page 46)
C. Without the use of the Extra Eye, the bus can be locked from the outside by children or vandals using a stick or similar object, creating a potential death trap!

Cord Door Lock

Dashboard

to door

This simple lock could be used with or instead of the bar lock on Page 46.

A heavy cord is attached to the dashboard and hooks over the door mechanism's handle by the driver's seat, as shown by the dotted line. Arrows show direction of travel as the door opens.

With a cord door lock in place, door B on Page 46 can sometimes be opened by removing a cotter pin under the bus, so a bar lock would still be needed on that one.

Free Bar Lock

Overhead views of each door type

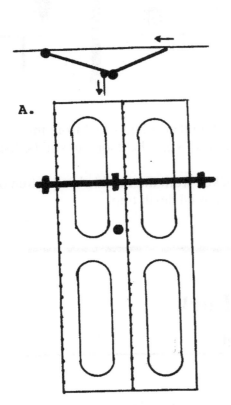

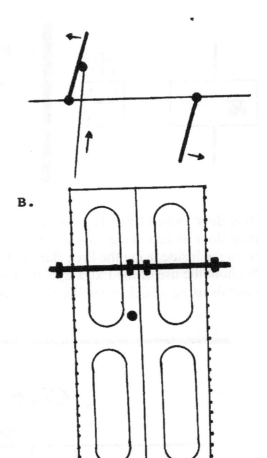

A.

B.

This illustration shows the mounting of the Free Bar Lock. To make one, cut a portion of the discarded overhead handrail and mount three or four of the hand rail hangers on the door and bus body as shown. The bus is unlocked by simply sliding the bar out of the hangers, toward the rear of the bus. The dot indicates the approximate location of the door opener mechanism. Dotted lines indicate hinges.

The top sketches are overhead views of each door type. Arrows indicate direction of travel of each component as the door is being opened. The position of the hangers is not shown in the overhead view.

A similar bar could be mounted on the rear door.

14. The sKOOLies
and Other Budget-friendly Conversions

Proof that fun
doesn't have to send you
to the poorhouse!

"Old Yeller"

(Well, it used to be yellow)

Dave's 1987 International is a 65-passenger, Thomas-built bus. It has a 6.9L diesel and a 5-speed transmission.

The bus features a queen-sized sofa bed in the rear, a single futon over one wheel well and three large bureaus.

The kitchen includes a three-burner stove with oven and double-bowl stainless steel sink. Two removed bus seats were used for the dinette.

across an old camp trailer from which he salvaged RV appliances. Some needed maintenance and cleaning, but the cost savings was significant. There are many such vehicles across America, some long since abandoned, from which you can often harvest otherwise expensive accessories.

Photos are courtesy of Dave Shea

The water tank holds 30 gallons with a 20 gallon gray water holding tank and a 6.2 gallon water heater. (Your holding tank capacity should exceed the fresh water supply, if practical.)

Electrical power includes:

- A 20-amp Converter (110v to 12v) mostly used to run lights.
- A 15-amp distribution panel with ground fault circuit breaker.
- Two deep-cycle 12-volt batteries run through a converter for auxiliary power.

Dave was fortunate enough to come

The Cool Bus

This simple set-up should secure the seat except in a major accident.

Photos of "The Cool Bus" in early stages of its conversion. The futon set-up would work well while stationary, but would be unsafe to use for seating on the road. The passenger would slide right off in an emergency stop.

Eric's 1977 International Harvester is powered by a 345 CID I.H. engine and has a five-speed transmission. Simple in design and appointment, even with the kitchen and bunks (not installed yet), the total investment was only $800.00 *including* the bus.

Hey, even I can afford that!

Perfect for camping or the beach.

The wall in front improves night driving and reduces road noise in the passenger area.

Photos are courtesy of Eric Curtis

Joreth's International Skoolie

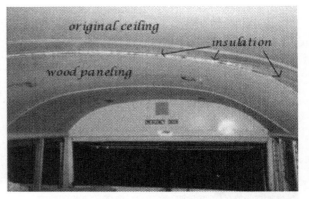

Before paneling the ceiling, Joreth used a very thin insulation that resembles bubble wrap covered in tin foil. While not as good as fiberglass or the new foam insulation, since a sKOOLie's roof is already very low, she wanted to keep the ceiling treatments thin. Because wood paneling tends to twist slightly when forced to fit the bus' curved ceiling, the panels didn't match up exactly, leaving small, uneven gaps between the panels. Joreth covered these seams with molding, resulting in an aesthetically pleasing and better insulated surface.

To provide for a straight, smooth, and better insulated straight side wall, Joreth installed a framework and plywood paneling. The bolts (left) were cut and capped when done, and with cabinets and features installed, were not visible.

50

Here Joreth is installing a framework of 2x4s on the floor. She cut and inserted pieces of 3-5 inch fiberglass insulation in the cavities and screwed 5/8-inch plywood over the top, compressing the insulation and forming a solid floor.

The disadvantage to this, of course, is with the already low ceiling of the typical sKOOLie, more than two inches of head room were lost. A single layer of ½" or ¾" plywood would have provided a smooth, level surface with less expense, less work and less loss of headroom.

Nearly ready to go. Joreth's sKOOLie is initially being used as a combination RV/moving van/ temporary quarters. This conversion has the beginnings of a well done sKOOLie.

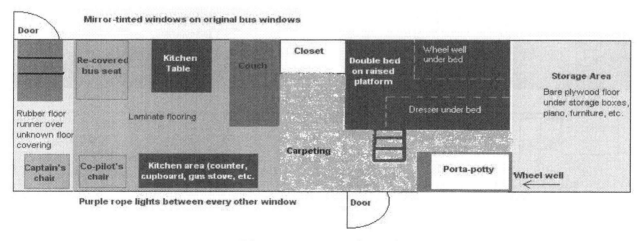

Photos courtesy of Joreth

Tony's 1981 International School Bus

Tony's bus is powered by an MV404 V-8 engine that had originally been powered by LP gas. Tony converted it to gasoline for easier fill-ups on the highway. The bus gets seven miles per gallon with 6 people and loaded to 25,000 pounds.

The interior includes a TV, VCR, Stereo, Microwave, Ice Box, Port-a-Potty, Closet, Sink, Two Couch/beds, a Dinette/bed, AC Inverter, Window and privacy curtains, tinted windows and even a Luxurious Oriental rug!

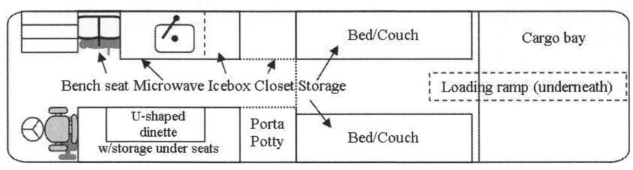

Bench seat Microwave Icebox Closet Storage

Bed/Couch

Cargo bay

Loading ramp (underneath)

U-shaped dinette w/storage under seats

Porta Potty

Bed/Couch

Locking pins for
when ramp is in use.

⇦ **Ramp storage**

The bus includes a nine-foot rear cargo bay that
can only be entered through the rear door. All
cargo bay windows have been painted black on
the inside for added security.

To facilitate loading band equipment, Tony
installed an aluminum ramp that mounts on a
framework under the bus and can be locked in
place so you don't lose it on the highway. The
circles above the ramp (top photo) show the
location of pins to lock the ramp in position
while in use.

This setup lends itself well to concessionaires
following carnivals as it provides both quarters
and inventory storage. You might consider
adding a door to the main cabin if you try this.

Photos are courtesy of Tony Basley.

Lauro Recendez' 1961 42 foot GM Bus

Lauro's Bus is powered by a 482 diesel V-8 with a manual transmission. Combining a good quality commercial bus with an economical conversion, this coach offers the best of both worlds. It features a kitchen, living area, two bunk beds, a bathroom and a large storage area in the rear.

This type of conversion is popular with vendors following fairs as it affords both lodging and storage space for inventory.

Photos are courtesy of Lauro Recendez

Bob bids you, "Welcome aboard *the Mountain Mist*"

Bob's Dodge Blue Bird was about 85% converted when he found it in a classified ad. It is powered by Dodge's famous 360 CID V-8 and a standard transmission.

He first became interested in conversions in 1972 when he had a VW Microbus. Always feeling cramped, Bob graduated to *the Mountain Mist,* which sleeps four and includes a full bath and kitchen with microwave, TV, VCR, inverter and even a back porch!

If you buy someone else's project, Bob suggests that make sure that you like what they have done. He doesn't care for the floor plan, but it was too late to alter it without major expense.

Photos are courtesy of Bob & Bev Post

The Sojourner

Being his fourth conversion, when Michael Pahl purchased this International sKOOLie he already had a complete set of plans and knew exactly what he was going to do. Using a unique design, commercial RV windows and entry door, he hoped to create an overall look that would put the Sojourner in a category of it's own. It was important to Michael that his new conversion be looked upon with respect rather than the negative image so many school bus conversions seem to have. To a large degree he succeeded, but there are those who will always look down their noses at a sKOOLie no matter what is done.

Michael started with a two-step roof and floor raise to provide for additional headroom, inside storage and most important of all, an inside shop and garage for his motorcycle without sacrificing living space.

The bus is top quality throughout and features teak parquet floors, tile counters and 1/4" mahogany plywood on the walls and ceiling.

Michael is already planning his fifth and final bus conversion, Sojourner 5, for his retirement years. It will feature an almost identical floor plan, but will be 43 feet long including a three foot patio on the back. We will be looking for it!

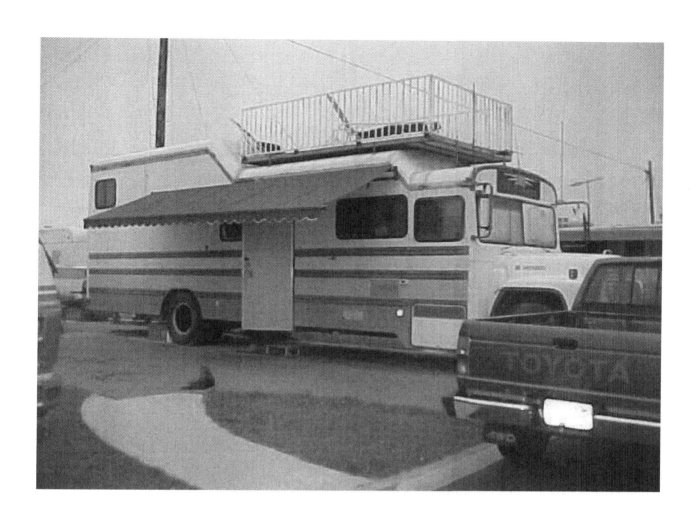

Not to scale

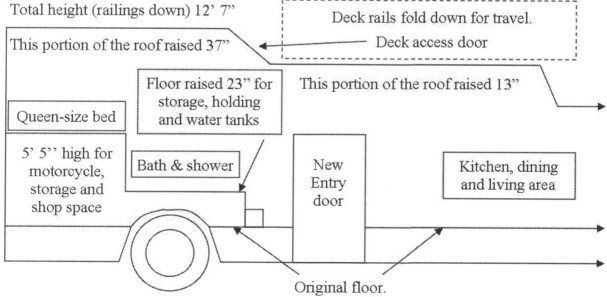

Total height (railings down) 12' 7"

This portion of the roof raised 37"

Deck rails fold down for travel.

Deck access door

Floor raised 23" for storage, holding and water tanks

This portion of the roof raised 13"

Queen-size bed

5' 5" high for motorcycle, storage and shop space

Bath & shower

New Entry door

Kitchen, dining and living area

Original floor.

Raising the roof. The center section was raised 13" and the rear section 37". The interior sheet metal was removed and the walls insulated with 1 1/2" Styrofoam obtained free from a local piano store. Total height (with patio rails down) is 12' 7".

Below: A generator now occupies the space left when the original stepwell was removed.

Access to the shop and storage area is through the double doors on the rear of the bus as well as a small door below the bed from inside. (See photo on page 60.) The modified original back door (above the double doors) provides emergency exit from the queen-size bed, if needed.

The smaller holding tank and storage area is open to the shop area and is also accessible through a trap door in the bathroom floor near the shower.

Michael cut a "slot" in the rear bumper (not shown) and installed a framework under the bus to hold an eight foot ramp which he uses to load his motorcycle.

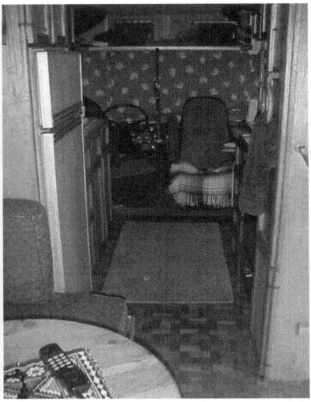

Top left. Living and dining area showing steps up to the bath area and master bedroom. The ladder leads to the deck above. The small door in the bathroom against the far wall leads to the shop below in the back of the bus. (See a better photo of the trap door below.)

Top right. The refrigerator and kitchen sink are on the left. The range, a pull out pantry, microwave and counters are on the right. The co-pilot's chair doubles as a computer station.

Left: Bath area and queen-size bed. The door under the bed leads to the shop in the rear of bus.

A second trap door in the floor by the shower provides access to the holding tanks and storage area. The round fixtures on the wall by the bed and toilet are forced air ducts for the furnace.

A Paloma instantaneous water heater and provides an unlimited amount of hot water on demand.

Above: Eight cubic foot refrigerator and tile counter. The sink's false drawer fronts are tip outs for silverware and other items. Cabinets are mahogany trim over mahogany plywood.

Below: Apartment size range is big enough for a 20 lb. turkey. The edge of a pull out pantry is barely seen in the lower right corner.

Living area. The ladder goes up to the deck. The dinette converts into a double bed and, with the settee opposite (not shown) and the queen size bed, this coach sleeps 5 comfortably.

"Thanks for stopping by. Come back again soon."

Photos are courtesy of Michael and Ginger Pahl

"Da Funky Bus"

Paul's sKOOLie is powered by a 392 International Engine with a 4-speed manual transmission and a dual speed rear end, which is a must for highway driving. It also has an oil bath air filter which is great for dusty states, plus there are no filters to buy.

Paul uses a 3000 Watt Inverter and four-six volt Golf Cart Batteries, two sets of two in series, each of which produces 12 volts. Then the two sets are wired in parallel to boost amperage output. `

Paul has been full timing for about three years now, and his coach is equipped with two bunks and a queen size bed, kitchen and bath.

To keep in touch while on the road, he also has a satellite dish with Internet access.

He uses a single holding tank for gray and black water.

Photos are courtesy of Paul Eastman

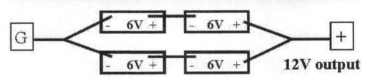

12V output

Ahhh – The 60s

**Some
cool sKOOLies from the
2000 Bus Conversion
Convention
in Laughlin, Nevada**

Old Airplane ⬇

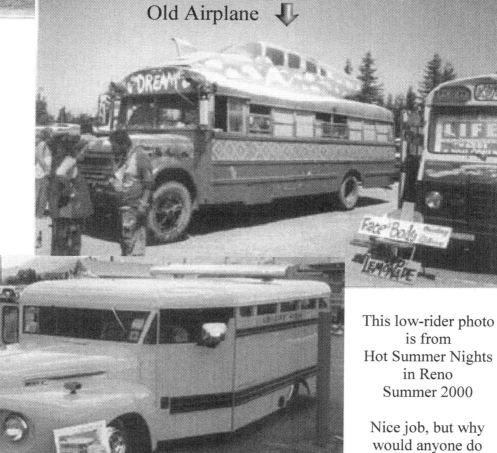

This low-rider photo
is from
Hot Summer Nights
in Reno
Summer 2000

Nice job, but why
would anyone do
this to a bus?

Solar Cooker ⬇

Glass Blowing Shop ⬇

Photos are courtesy of Angel and Dave McNall

66

15. The StratoCruisers

When you can afford
to do it right!

Bart's "Down Under" 1985 Nissan

Bart's bus is a 1985 Nissan DA67 coach imported from Japan to New Zealand. It is roughly 40 feet long and 12 feet high. A lot of that height is luggage space so Bart decided to raise the roof another six inches to provide adequate ceiling height.

Although doing much of the work himself, Bart hired a coach design company to raise the roof and he contracted for the finish work like cabinetry, carpeting and tile work

His careful planning and attention to detail resulted in a superb full-time live-in conversion. Bart designed the conversion in 3D with a modeling program called Design Workshop Lite. Design Workshop Lite is free and can be downloaded from **http://www.artifice.com/.**

Photos are courtesy of Bart Kindt

More than 4400 lbs. of material were removed.

Raising the roof 15 Centimeters (roughly six inches)

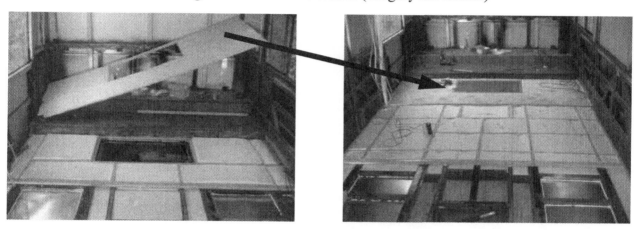

After installing water tanks and other prep work,
the floor was fully insulated and resurfaced section by section.
Left and right photos show progression with insulation and plywood sub-floor placement.

Front stairwell

Before

⬅

After

Ready for
carpet

➡

Tabletops, in the kitchen, bath and bedroom are from solid Remu, a native New Zealand hardwood.

The tops are made by gluing pieces of Remu wood together. Then, with a lot of sanding and spraying, you get an awesome result.

Pull-out Pantry

Kitchen

Tile bath and shower.

The large bathroom mirror behind the vanity gives the feeling of spaciousness. Note the Remu wood vanity top.

(Wish my home looked this good!)

Beautiful Remu counter top.

Solar panels

The bus electrical system features

- an 1100 amp/hour battery pack (6 – 12 volt 1100 amp/hour batteries in series)
- A 2500 watt inverter/charger/control system (Trace Engineering, US),
- Solar charging control system (Trace)
- and 9 - 80 watt solar panels on the roof...
- An extra 12 volt/130 amp alternator on the front of the engine.
- A 7-Kilowatt diesel generator

Bart can charge the batteries four ways:
- Shore power or the
- Generator with the inverter,
- alternator when the engine runs (130 Amps)
- Solar panels (45 Amps with full sun, about 10 Amps on a cloudy day.)

Miller's Detroit Diesel

Don't judge a book by its cover. It is not uncommon to see RVs covered with a tarp in the "back 40."

Miller's bus is powered by a Detroit Diesel pusher engine and a new Allison transmission. This beautifully appointed conversion is road worthy and has all the comforts of home.

The full kitchen features gas range and oven, built-in microwave, refrigerator with freezer, washer and dryer, a double sink and even a built-in coffee maker!

The dinette has bench seating with storage underneath. The coach has 100 gallons of fresh water on board and huge holding tanks making extended RVing a breeze..

Other features include:

- Two electrical power sources – one 12-volt DC system and a 110-volt AC system with a 2100 watt power inverter and roof-mounted roof solar panels
- Air conditioner with heat strip and one 12-volt swamp cooler.
- Sleeps six with one double bed in bedroom, a hide-a-bed and one drop down bed.
- Complete bathroom with toilet, shower and sink.
- Walk-in closet. Living area with sofa and loveseat.
- CB radio
- Nine inch TV/monitor and rear view camera mounted in rear of RV to assist in backing up.
- 85 feet of overhead cabinet storage and additional storage in "The Basement" around the outside of the RV.
- Water heater
- Floor furnace (with thermostat) provides heating throughout.

Photos are courtesy of Mr. and Mrs. Donald Miller.

Jim's '57 Detroit Diesel

Jim Sims of Pensacola Florida is the owner of this beautiful 1957 PD4104. It features a 671 Detroit diesel 6 in good shape with a 4-speed transmission and gets about ten miles to the gallon.

The coach sleeps six and is equipped with an RV refrigerator with an ice maker, a separate freezer, built in vacuum and two air conditioners. It is finished with light oak with blue trim and parquet floor has cedar closets.

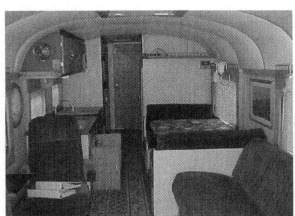

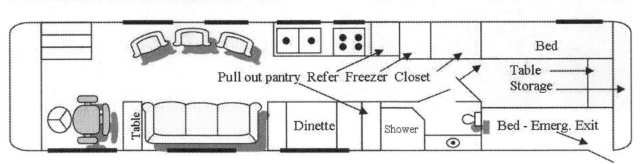

Note trim work on headliner (above) in the driver's compartment. This unmatched attention to detail is evident throughout the coach.

The intricate oak "railing" type trim work (bottom left photo) is used throughout the coach on window sills and shelving.

Photos are courtesy of James Sims

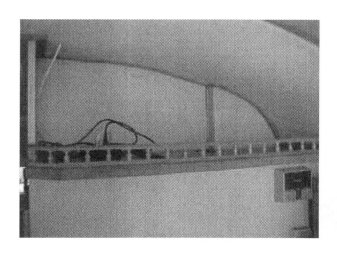

"Cal" McClure's 1948 Gillig

Cal's 1948 Gillig is a 35-foot diesel pusher.

The driver and co-pilots seats are from an old Corvair. Note the convenient folding table (shown folded down) in front of the co-pilot.

The **reclining twin beds**, immediately behind the driver, double as lounges chairs. Hinged in the center, each end can fold up, facing forward while on the road, or aft when parked. A table is placed between them for dining, and can comfortably seat six adults. Plans for these reclining twin beds included are in Cal's book, ***How to Build Low Cost Motorhomes***.

The kitchen area features a double-bowl sink and more counter area than most RVs. An 8 cubic foot household refrigerator freezer is just behind the range.

In addition to the drawers and cupboards below the counter, overhead cabinets line both walls.

Looking aft (below) you will note elevated twin beds in the rear of the bus. A long drawer is under each, providing convenient storage.

On the wall above the range is a gas light. On mild evenings, it provides all the heat they need.

Originally designed with a convertible dinette, as the McClure's needs changed, they removed the dinette in favor of a more casual lounge area. Swivel chairs and a folding table create a relaxed setting.

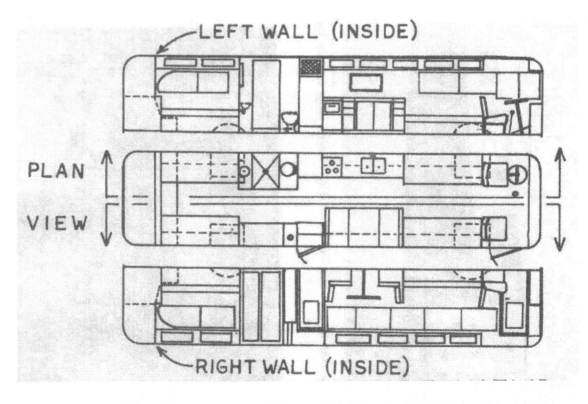

LEFT WALL (INSIDE)

PLAN

VIEW

RIGHT WALL (INSIDE)

Photos are courtesy of Mr. and Mrs. Louis C. McClure

The DAFfy Canuck

Before and after photos

The DAFfy Canuck is a 1969 bus manufactured in Roeselare, Belgium by Carrosserie-Jonckheere for DAF.

The Lawrence's started by raising the roof seven inches, starting behind the driver's seat.

Framing was welded in place on 16" centers,

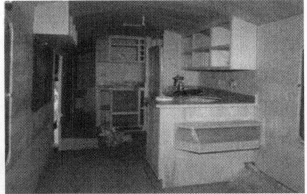

3/4" Foil covered rigid polyurethane insulation was cut and press fit between each frame. A second layer was separated by a spacer, creating dead air space as well as space for electrical wiring in the walls and ceiling.

All paneling was Baltic Birch as it has a very fine grain and leaves a smooth finish when painted resembling Formica.

Note the raceway (bottom left photo.) This provides a channel for electrical wiring and pipe.

Bedroom before and after.

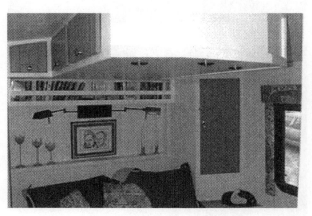

Top left and right. Before and after kitchen photos. Note the raceway (top left) for plumbing and wiring.

Bottom left and right. Kitchen cabinets before and after. Note ample counter space.

Features

General:
Overall dimensions: 36' 6" x 96 inches.
466 International six cylinder with exhaust brake and an Allison five speed transmission.

Power:
- Coach power totally 120v supplied by trace 4024, 4000 watt inverter. (24-volt)
- Four Trojan six-volt 220ah batteries. (series/parallel 24-volt)
- Battery equalizer - 12-volt accessories
- 2 Siemens ProCharger 4JF 75-watt solar panels in series (24v)
- 24 Volt AIR 403, 400 watt wind charger
- 8 kw Kubota 3 cylinder diesel powered genset

Water:
- 120 imperial gallons in two tanks
- 80 imperial gallons grey water
- 40 imperial gallons black water (All tanks are made from 1/4" white ABS plastic.)

Other features:
- Suburban 42,000 BTU propane furnace.
- Dometic RM7030 Side by Side Fridge Freezer, with ice maker. 110-volt/LPG.
- 1000w Microwave oven
- Propane 4 burner and oven.
- Corner Sink.

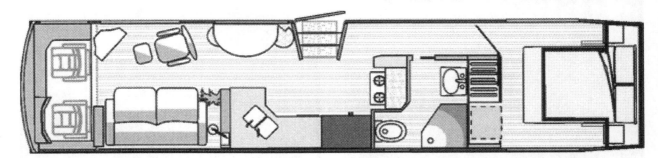

Photos are courtesy of Myrna and Jim Lawrence.

Our old red '64 Dodge conversion (Above)
"Grace" when we brought her home (below)

Finding Grace
By Dave and Angel McNall

Dave and Angel McNall

We first came across our bus while living in a house in Reseda, California. We had vacationed many years in an old '64 Dodge camper (left top) built by Dave's grandfather, and had always enjoyed the simpler, more mobile lifestyle. We have traveled across the country in it, even on our honeymoon! It seemed that every time we were on the road in our camper we had everything we needed and more; we never thought of our house.

Nearing the end of our trip, the prospect of returning home always made us sad. We had a great house in a lovely neighborhood, but the cost of living was high, and not only did we not *need* all of that space and stuff, we felt tied down.

One day, Dave was browsing the classified ads and saw an ad for a '66 Bluebird, partially converted, for $3300. It was sitting in a storage yard, where it had been abandoned for the last nine years. We went to look at it immediately.

It wasn't much to look at from the outside-just a huge yellow school bus with enormous panels of rusty metal where the sides had been cut and the roof raised. It still said Garden Grove unified School District No. 57 on the side. Because the people selling had purchased it at a lien sale, it had no keys so we couldn't start it or even open the doors.

There was a chair sitting nearby and, after we climbed up on it, we got the back window open. We hoisted ourselves through the window and fell onto a musty old mattress inside the bus. When I looked up I could not believe my eyes! It was the most beautiful bus I had ever seen, and we'd been in some really nice homemade conversions during our time on the road!

The walls and ceiling were beautifully paneled in oak and cedar and there were so many cabinets! The roof had been raised and it was very spacious inside, with sunlight streaming in from the three sunroofs.

The bus already had a full bath with shower, and a complete kitchen with a brand new three way refrigerator, range and oven, including the original paperwork!

We wanted this bus badly, but where would we park it?! We already had a big red school bus in our back yard that we were working on and we had a *long* way to go. Lucky for us, we had really great neighbors that didn't mind our giant bus out by the side of our house. At least they claimed not to mind.

After we made arrangements to purchase the bus, we installed a new battery, changed the oil and fluids, added some fresh fuel, and she started right up – after sitting for nine years!

Although the bus was already about 75% converted, there was still a lot of work to do. Registration was the first major hurdle. The bus had no title, registration, pink slip, manuals, receipts, or any of the usual paperwork necessary for transferring the title. We couldn't even find the Vehicle Identification Number. Finally, the CHP assigned us a new VIN and we got our title and plates, "N2Grace." We felt that it was by the Grace of God that we found this beautiful new

home that would enable us to pursue our dream.

With ownership finally established, we went right to work. I sanded and refinished all of the wood in the bus, finding quite a few nasty water stains. Dave finished all of the electrical and plumbing. Next, Dave went to work on the engine and auxiliary generator and bought new tires and batteries.

We laid down a linoleum floor. It looks like wood in the front and back, and we have green tiles in the kitchen.

I am a chef and wanted the kitchen to be a special area, separated from the rest of the bus. We built in sliding cabinet racks that help me keep all of my pots and appliances organized, and a double basin stainless-steel sink.

IKEA was a great source of organizational tools. They also have lights that run off of 12 volts if you remove the transformer. We bought several because the fancy RV lights just weren't our style.

We felt that a full size couch was important so we searched high and low for one that would fit through a school bus door. We finally found a beautiful La-Z-Boy sofa at a Sears outlet store. It has a panel in the middle that folds down for a little table, and the ends incline.

The best part, though, was when we were getting ready to take it home. As we were trying to fit it through the door, the sales guy says, "do

you want me to take the back off for you?"
It actually separated in two pieces, the seat,
and the back cushions. Perfect fit!

We needed some sort of table in the living
area, but didn't want to take up too much
space. What we came up with was two tables
that are mounted on the wall and fold down
when we don't want them there. We also
have two tall thin chairs that fold up.

The driver and passenger seats were bought
second hand from an RV salvage yard, and
after cleaning were as good as new. Two
dogs and a kitty live with us, so we went
with some nice throw rugs instead of carpet
and I made window curtains. They are pretty
and clean up much easier than mini blinds. I
don't even have to iron them.

Then we had the bus painted.

We still have many things that we want to
do, such as covering our dash with wood, and
some day putting in a "real" front door, but
for now it's perfect.

To anyone who may be considering this
lifestyle, we say *go for it*! Living in a bus is
wonderful. We spend a lot more time in
nature, and because it costs so much less to
support ourselves, we have more time and
energy enjoy the things that really matter in
life.

Most people we meet express the wish that
they could live this way, but think they need
a lot of stuff. We gave away 80% of our
"stuff" and still have way more than we
need. The best part is that we are following
our dreams. Life is too short not to do the
things that make you happy. God blessed us
with Grace and now we will keep on truckin'
down whatever path He leads us.

Grace

'66 Bluebird Pusher

- 36' Long, 8' wide, 11'7'' Tall (Inside 7'6")
- 478 CID gas engine
- 5-Speed manual transmission
- 5.6 KW Onan Generator
- 120-12-volt converter and charger
- A/C – central air (Ducted)
- Heat – forced air (Ducted)
- Water heater – Rinnai instant hot water
- Refrigerator – Dometic RM1303
- Range/Oven, microwave
- Full size shower
- King size bed
- Satellite TV, wired for phone
- Laptop With DSL connection
- Stereo W/ surround sound / home theater
- 21' awning with California room

King size bed in rear of "Grace"

"Grace" today

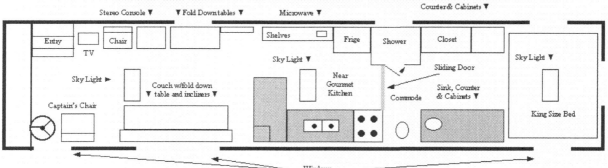

Photos are courtesy of Dave and Angel McNall

16. Gypsy Caravans

The Father of the Modern RV

Why a chapter on Gypsy Caravans in a Bus Conversion book? Well, when you think about it, the caravan is a predecessor to the bus conversion and its owners are near kin.

The Gypsies faced the same challenges we do today, space and weight, and their solutions were no less innovative than are ours.

Caravans were not widely used by Gypsies until the mid nineteenth century, where they started out as little more than tent structures on a wheeled platform. By the 1880s the Gypsies in all parts of Britain had become the world's greatest users of mobile homes, retaining this pre-eminence for the next sixty years. During its brief reign, the Gypsy caravan became the symbol of the carefree spirit and the adventure and romance of the open road.

The Gypsies' homes on wheels ranged from the very modest, inexpensive units, like today's sKOOLies, to the most

elaborate, ornate palaces on wheels.

One of the more luxurious vans, the Reading, was mainly ordered by wealthy horse dealers and Gypsy kings or queens, the upper crust of Romany society. The carving and scrollwork of the porches were extremely elaborate.

Furniture was built into the interiors and often included two china cabinets with glass doors, a three drawer dresser, settee and a stove which was used primarily for heating. (Most gypsies preferred to cook and eat outdoors when weather permitted.)

The parent's bed extended from across the back of the wagon and had a space for young children underneath. Older children slept outside, under the wagon. In good weather, the entire family usually slept outside.

The "pan box" was attached to the wagon under the floor between the rear wheels and was used for storing cast iron pans to keep

suety pans from soiling the interior.

The curtains were of silk, satin or velvet, trimmed at the borders with lace, crochet work or tufted bobbles. All interior decorating followed the Victorian style that was popular at the time. Even the china cabinets were filled with the finest quality Victorian china available at the time.

Much hand carving was done for both utility and decorative effect, especially the chamfering of the uprights and chief members of the bodywork, which decreased overall weight without sacrificing strength.

Carvings on doors, porch brackets and weatherboards, on the other hand, were purely decorative. In the larger vans all of the supporting members including the ribs and undercarriage members were chamfered, gilded painted and pinstriped. The amount of carving and gilding was indicative of the wealth of the family.

The vans were painted in bright colors, primarily maroon or dark red, a lighter and brighter red with more orange in its composition, a medium green and a strong yellow. Other colors such as lighter greens, purple, blue and violet were used for small details incidental to the main theme and rarely, if ever, for large areas of body or upper works. White, pale yellow or gray colors for the bodywork were described by gypsies as "poverty colors". Hmmm... I wonder if "pale yellow" was a predecessor to "school bus yellow?"

Like the Gypsies of yesterday, conversion owners are seen by many as "a bit odd." If you feel self conscious, just reflect on your heritage and take comfort in the fact that you are in good company.

Modern "RV" Park. Hey, no hook-up fees!

Photos courtesy of:

Wally Roth,
Gypsy Vans by Roth,
"Builder of Collector Quality
Gypsy Vans"

Visit their website for more information at:
http://www.gypsyvans.com/

17. Potpourri and Adios

Over the years I have visited with scores of home converters and checked out countless conversions. Each one was unique and incorporated the owner's ideas and designs. Some of these ideas were, well, "not-so-good."

My old history professor used to say, "those who won't learn from history are doomed to repeat it." With this in mind, I present an hodge-podge of my most memorable observations for your consideration and amusement.

Case Study No. 1. "Free Spirit", a '65 GMC conversion features several interesting ideas, some good, some not so good. Anyway, it's a good place to start.

Gravity-feed water system. Where, oh, where to put the water tank? Hey, if you put it on the roof, you won't need a water pump, right? Well, not exactly. The problem is, a hundred gallons of water will add unnecessary stress to the roof, not to mention the instability created by that much shifting water well above the center of gravity when navigating turns. Also, think of the constant slosh, splash, gurgle, slosh.

Rattling cabinets. Need an extra cabinet above the sink? The same people who brought you the "gravity feed water system" also installed a nifty cabinet from an old house made of heavy-duty sheet metal. Not really a problem, except... well, the doors were also made of the same sheet metal. They were sliding doors. Loose sliding doors. Every time you hit a bump...

Stairwell trap door. Their one good idea was sort of a trap door. They used a piece of plywood to cover the stairwell, creating floor space when the bus is on the road.

The only real danger here would be in case of accident. No one from the outside would be able to open a standard bus door, it would jam because part of the door folds inward. In their case, they replaced the old school bus door with a standard house type door, so it worked out OK. When parked or in traffic, the "door" could be removed and stowed away. (If using a house door, ensure that the glass is safety glass.)

Case Study No. 2. Motorcycle loading ramp. Pat Macumber of San Diego built a ramp for loading his motorcycles inside the bus. He started by cutting a "slot" in the rear bumper approximately 4" high and 16" wide. Under the bus, he built a framework between the bus' "I" beams that lined up with the slot. All he had to do when he got to his destination was unlock the ramp, slide it out and set it into position on a mounting bracket installed just below the rear door. A similar ramp is described on Page 53.

Case Study No. 3. Bunk bed converts to sofa. John Brandes of San Diego had a small truck conversion. To conserve precious space, he designed his bunk beds to double as seating. The lower bunk was installed at normal seat height. The upper bunk was hinged at the back and, when not in use, folded DOWN forming the back of the newly created sofa. At bedtime, all he had to do was lift the upper bunk into place, insert a pin in the wall at one end and attach the brace to the other.

Case Study No. 4. Look out for junk!

After seeing some of the variety of buses available you might want to take some advice from Donald Morris of Plantsville, Connecticut. He spent several months looking in four states before finding his coach. "There is definitely a lot of junk out there with high price tags," he says, "The first thing I would recommend is not to be in a hurry to buy the first thing that comes along." Sound advice!

In one respect, a bus is just like a car, a tool, an appliance, or any other commodity: If it looks too good to be true, it probably is. While there sometimes are real bargains or genuine "distress sales," saving a few bucks in the initial purchase will very likely cost you *big* when it comes time to make repairs. Any mechanic will tell you that the most expensive tool you can buy is a cheap one, because you have to buy it twice—once for the initial purchase, the second time to replace an inferior product, preferably with a quality tool this time. And a $20.00 tool is chump change when compared with a $5,000 bus!

Here's another way to think about it. The bus is merely a mobile platform for your conversion. You can <u>easily</u> spend $10,000 on the conversion alone, not to mention hundreds or thousands of man-hours. If the platform can't perform, or will only last a season or two, that is a lot of money to leave sitting in your driveway. On the other hand, if you really do need a place to house your mother-in-law...

The best advice I can give you comes to me over and over again from bus nuts, experienced converters and just plain common sense: *Buy the best platform you can afford!* It doesn't have to be the newest or the shiniest or the cleanest or have the lowest mileage, but it must be in the best mechanical and structural condition possible. Have the coach thoroughly checked out before getting emotionally involved with it. It will help save your pocket book, your sanity and possibly even your marriage.

Postscript

Originally only 16 pages in 1982, this booklet has gone through a score of changes and revisions.

We have enjoyed several trips and had much pleasure from our bus. The mistakes we made and lessons we learned the hard way have been detailed so you might learn from our errors.

We wish you success in your venture and many carefree years of enjoyment from your bus.

Thank you,

Ben Rosander
PO Box 327
Marysville, WA 98270-0327

http://www.rv-busconversions.com/

Email: ben@rv-busconversions.com

Appendix

These are a few of the many bus conversion books available today. If your bookstore doesn't stock them, you can order them on-line at **http://www.rv-busconversions.com/** or write for a free bus conversion book catalog to:

Ben Rosander
PO Box 327
Marysville, WA 98270-0327

If you know of other bus conversion books or materials, please contact me. Thank you.

Bus Conversion
Floor Plans,
by Ben Rosander

Dreams on Wheels:
Modern Do-it-Yourself
Gypsies
by Ben Rosander

How to Build
Low Cost Motorhomes
by Louis C. McClure

The Bus Pages
A Yellow Pages
style reference
book for the bus
industry

The Bus
Converter's
Bible
by Dave Galey

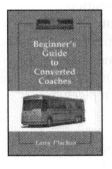

Beginner's Guide
to Converted
Coaches,
by Larry Plachno

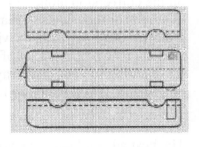

Bus Conversion
Floor Planner Kits

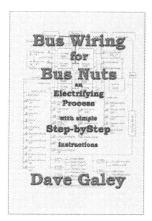

***Bus Wiring for
Bus Nuts***
by Dave Galey

***Classy Cabinets
for Converted
Coaches***
by Dave Galey

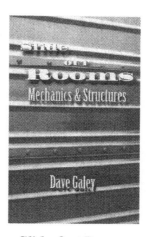

***Slide Out Rooms,
Mechanics and
Structures***
by Dave Galey

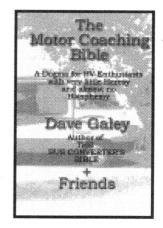

***The
Motor Coaching
Bible***
by Dave Galey

NFPA 1192 Standard on Recreational Vehicles

This book is a <u>MUST HAVE</u> for ANYONE attempting a home bus conversion.

This book can be ordered from the National Fire Protection Assn. at **http://www.nfpa.org**

Periodicals

These magazines are available at a discount through
http://www.rv-busconversions.com/rvmagazines.html

Bus Conversions

Motorhome

Trailer Life

Gypsy Journal

Index

CPSIA information can be obtained at www.ICGtesting.com
Printed in the USA
LVOW020011010713
340919LV00001B/23/A